Praise for *Outward Bound Lessons to Live a Life of Leadership*

"Mark provides a vision for the kind of leader that we should each want to be and that our culture desperately needs. This book will leave you inspired and eager to become an Expeditionary Leader!"

—Ryan Barton, founder and CEO, Mainstay Technologies

"In this book, Compassionate Leadership is clearly defined as an indispensable approach to removing obstacles that prevent one from achieving one's full potential. By highlighting the Outward Bound experiences of others, Mark reaffirms the importance of acknowledging how stories matter and how important it is for leaders to take the time to understand the *why* behind the *what* of an individual's professional and personal endeavors."

—Donato Tramuto, CEO, Tivity Health; founder and President, Health eVillages; and author of *Life's Bulldozer Moments*

"I will never forget my Outward Bound experience and Mark Brown. My company at the time was investing in its leaders and provided twelve of us the opportunity to join Mark on a three-day Outward Bound adventure. I was a bit intimidated at the thought of being in the wild with nine men and one other woman, but I learned that there was no reason for that apprehension. Instead, I learned more about myself in those three days than I would have ever imagined. Meeting with Mark on a regular basis after those three days was just as dramatic. He was able to help me with clarity on what I learned and how I could take that life lesson to mold my future. My Outward Bound trip took place seventeen years ago, and it was a turning point for me and my future direction. It significantly impacted my life. The lessons in this book can do the same for you. Thanks, Mark, for being such a huge part of my life journey."

—Jen Tolbert, Regional Vice President, Sales, Cornerstone OnDemand

Outward Bound

Outward Bound

Lessons to Live a Life of

Leadership

To Serve, to Strive, and Not to Yield

by **Mark Michaux Brown**

Foreword by **Richard Leider**

Berrett–Koehler Publishers, Inc.

Berrett-Koehler Publishers, Inc.   Tel: (510) 817-2277
1333 Broadway, Suite 1000   Fax: (510) 817-2278
Oakland, CA 94612-1921   www.bkconnection.com

ORDERING INFORMATION

Quantity sales. Special discounts are available on quantity purchases by corporations, associations, and others. For details, contact the "Special Sales Department" at the Berrett-Koehler address above.

Individual sales. Berrett-Koehler publications are available through most bookstores. They can also be ordered directly from Berrett-Koehler: Tel: (800) 929-2929; Fax: (802) 864-7626; www.bkconnection.com.

Orders for college textbook / course adoption use. Please contact Berrett-Koehler: Tel: (800) 929-2929; Fax: (802) 864-7626.

Distributed to the US trade and internationally by Penguin Random House Publisher Services.

Berrett-Koehler and the BK logo are registered trademarks of Berrett-Koehler Publishers, Inc.

Printed in the United States of America.

Berrett-Koehler books are printed on long-lasting acid-free paper. When it is available, we choose paper that has been manufactured by environmentally responsible processes. These may include using trees grown in sustainable forests, incorporating recycled paper, minimizing chlorine in bleaching, or recycling the energy produced at the paper mill.

Library of Congress Cataloging-in-Publication Data

Names: Michaux Brown, Mark, author.
Title: Outward bound lessons to live a life of leadership : to serve, to strive, and not to
    yield / Mark Michaux Brown.
Description: First Edition. | Oakland, CA : Berrett-Koehler Publishers, 2019.
Identifiers: LCCN 2019015832 | ISBN 9781523098309 (paperback)
Subjects: LCSH: Leadership. | Self-reliance. | Motivation (Psychology) | BISAC: BUSINESS
    & ECONOMICS / Motivational. | BUSINESS & ECONOMICS / Leadership.
Classification: LCC HD57.7.M523 2019 | DDC 158/.4—dc23
LC record available at https://lccn.loc.gov/2019015832

First Edition   25 24 23 22 21 20 19   10 9 8 7 6 5 4 3 2 1

Book producer and text designer: Leigh McLellan Design
Cover designer: Rob Johnson, Toprotype, Inc.
Cover image © Outward Bound

Contents

SECTION III **Not to Yield** 71

The Expeditionary Leader

J ust two words capture what I would like to say to introduce the book that follows: *Rx: To Serve.* The Outward Bound motto— To Serve, to Strive, and Not to Yield—has always struck a deep chord within me. And, if there is one great secret to becoming an Expeditionary Leader, it is to never give up on giving—to serve.

Life has a way of bringing you back to places that you thought that you had left for good. And I keep coming back to Outward Bound. But my relationship with Outward Bound is a proxy one. I don't claim to have ever been a student on a program (and part of me wishes I really had). But my connection, nevertheless, is deep.

I have served three terms on the Voyageur Outward Bound board of trustees. It was a trustee trek to climb Mount Kilimanjaro that opened up my deep forty-year relationships in Tanzania. And it was after that experience that I was inspired to create Voyageur Outward Bound's inaugural adult course—Life Career Renewal.

The lives of both of my children, Greta and Andrew, have been shaped by their Outward Bound experiences. In fact, Andrew served as the associate program director for Outward Bound in Montana and today continues to consult with Outward Bound leadership.

When I attend Outward Bound gatherings, I gain a renewed sense of the shared affection and connection that alumni feel. And it gets me reflecting on how their experience could have such an impact, often fifty years later.

My theory for that feeling is "expeditionary leaders." Enter Mark Brown. As he reflects in the book: "I have so many memories of that experience, but what stood out most of all to me was the demeanor and presence of my leaders. . . . I didn't know what it was they had. I only knew that I wanted it." The end of that first course was the beginning of his lifelong quest—the journey to discover what they had.

Mark starts honorably with his own story and challenges. Then he shares the stories of others who are mirrors of serving, striving, and not yielding. This book is a call to discover these possibilities in ourselves to set our own sails "outward bound."

Courage is the gateway to freedom, to fulfilling your life's work, and to answering the call to lead. Courage is the choice to do something that frightens you and that stretches your capability and capacity to grow and give. Courage is the constant companion in Outward Bound and in Mark's writing. Without it, you'll not take the first step toward your calling. Finding courage is a daily practice. What do you need the companionship of courage for? Read this book as your companion to truly up your courage factor.

> Richard Leider
> Bestselling author, *The Power of Purpose*

The Modern World Needs a New Model for Change

If you do not change direction,
you may end up where you are heading.
—Lao-Tzu

apid change defines our modern culture and lives. Technological advances occur at a lightning pace, rendering much of what we learn obsolete nearly as quickly as we learn it. We struggle to keep up with the ever-changing landscape, often leaving us in a state of disequilibrium. Some scientists have proposed that our activity has actually issued in a new geologic epoch called the Anthropocene, the time of humans. Our success as a species is altering the very landscape in which we live.

All our institutions, from small businesses and nonprofits to large multinational corporations and governments, are under tremendous stress. The advances that have fueled "the time of humans" have also created unintended and unpredictable consequences. The founders of our social media companies and the manufacturers of our handheld devices did not plan on the Arab Spring, terrorist-encrypted messages, or screen addiction. Our transportation and fuel industries didn't anticipate or intend that downtown Miami and scores of other coastal cities would be underwater at high tide as a result of rising seas caused by our energy consumption. And as we continue to embrace advances in artificial intelligence and machine learning, we will undoubtedly face unforeseeable side effects. At a recent conference I attended, a leader on the IBM Watson project declared that the next five years would have a greater impact on our world than the past ninety-five. How can we thrive in such turbulence?

The skills and knowledge that once meant a stable career now leave many people ill equipped for an ever-changing present. Many people feel left behind. It is like being on a roller coaster that never ends.

The truth is, we are still much like the explorers of early human history, in that we can see little of what lies beyond the horizon. But like those courageous adventurers, we are taking a look at the big unknown before us and setting our sails "outward bound." We are leaving the safety of our harbor and sailing into a future with no map. Safe passage requires skills, leadership, and action. The ship we sail is our only home, and our future depends on our navigation. The horizon line is behind us. We cannot go back.

How can we safely journey through this perilous time without clear knowledge of what we will face? Put into a modern context: How can we allow the tremendous creativity and advancement that capitalism fosters without exploiting our world and the people who inhabit it? How can we balance the tremendous freedom that our democratic experiment has created with a deeper sense of inclusion for all members of our society? How can we create a future where humanity can thrive and all of us can share in the advances of this new era?

The answers to these questions lie in the qualities of those who lead us. Today's leaders need vastly different abilities and approaches to guide tomorrow's institutions. Skills once deemed "soft" are now seen as crucial to success in the modern workplace. Once left to the fringes of social science and human resources, these people skills are now at the forefront of what is necessary to succeed as a leader and an employee. If in fact we have moved into the "age of humans," it follows that to thrive, we need leaders who are experts in unleashing human potential.

It makes sense then to turn to a leadership approach that was born in adversity and that recognizes disequilibrium and uncertainty as an integral part of business, personal, and political life. This approach is modeled by the Expeditionary Leader who sets sail "outward bound"—and who is willing and able to step outside conventional wisdom and use a deeply held set of core values and an understanding of human psychology to navigate uncharted waters and make a positive impact in the world.

Where Does Outward Bound Fit In?

Outward Bound is an international network of experience-based learning and leadership programs for youth and adults. An Outward Bound wilderness expedition begins with a small group leaving the safety of their world for the unknown wilderness, inevitably encountering difficulty and challenges. No one knows exactly what will happen, and all who participate must learn to navigate the uncertainty and the rapidly changing circumstances that nature presents. Along the way participants gain wisdom and are transformed. These expeditioners then bring that wisdom to their communities, uplifting and teaching those around them what they themselves have learned. It is this experience that creates Expeditionary Leaders.

Although Outward Bound as an educational organization began by leading groups into the wilderness, in the decades since its inception it has incorporated its principles and methods into everything from public school reform to leadership development at some of the world's leading corporations.

This book explores the process of becoming an Expeditionary Leader through the stories of people whose lives were touched by Outward Bound and who then went on to make a positive difference in the world. Some were leaders in Outward Bound; others were participants in its programs. Some names you may recognize. All share a zeal for making the world a better place and the grit to believe that they can. All have wisdom to impart gleaned from their years at Outward Bound and the years since, when they've had the opportunity to implement that wisdom.

To Serve, to Strive, and Not to Yield

Outward Bound's motto—To Serve, to Strive, and Not to Yield—is adapted from the final lines of Alfred Lord Tennyson's poem *Ulysses:*

> Tho' much is taken, much abides; and tho'
> We are not now that strength which in old days
> Moved earth and heaven, that which we are, we are;
> One equal temper of heroic hearts,
> Made weak by time and fate, but strong in will
> To strive, to seek, to find, and not to yield.

Time and again, those whom I interviewed for this book referenced that motto: To Serve, to Strive, and Not to Yield. To me, it represents the key that unlocks the Expeditionary Leader in all of us.

To Serve   Imagine workplaces focused on the well-being of their employees, their customers, their communities, and the greater world above all else. Imagine elected officials and civil servants who approach governing with compassion and a servant's heart, and who share a set of operating principles that include an ever-widening range of diversity.

To Strive   Imagine communities filled with people who see challenges as opportunities to grow, who value their own learning and mastery of skills as ways to contribute to the greater good. Imagine leaders at all levels and in all organizations who are willing to step out on a limb to do the right thing, who go the extra mile to ensure a better outcome.

Not to Yield   Imagine people who model compassion, integrity, and excellence despite the adversity they face at every turn. Imagine corporate leaders who take on the risks of putting people and planet first, knowing that a successful business is about playing the long game, not quarterly profits. Imagine if moral courage and integrity were taught as the expectation of society.

What would the world look like if we built all our institutions on such a foundation? This possibility is what Expeditionary Leadership unlocks.

I structured this book around these three keys of Expeditionary Leadership, based on the Outward Bound motto. Section 1 is about service, the idea that the strength of leadership is measured by a deep sense of purpose and aligning that call with a positive impact on others. Section 2 is about striving—that constant yearning to learn more, to do better, and to be better. Section 3 is about never yielding, knowing that the finish line is forever in the distance and that the best part of the expedition is always yet to come—just beyond the next challenge. It's also about standing true to your principles regardless of external pressures.

Those are the lessons I have had the privilege of learning in my years with Outward Bound. They have served me well in my professional and personal life. I have taken them with me into the various adventures of my life, and although I never knew where I would end up, I felt confident I had the key to unlock the door of transformation and positive impact wherever I went.

These lessons are told in this book through the stories of other Expeditionary Leaders—former Outward Bound leaders and participants who have left their mark on the world.

I have also included a critical component of experiential learning at the end of each chapter: pausing and reflecting on a situation, drawing out the learning, and then applying it. What I ask is that you reflect on each lesson and how it applies to your life, how you can use these learnings to unlock the Expeditionary Leader inside of you, just as the other leaders in this book have.

What Can These Keys Unlock?

"I liken it to carrying a magical key in your pocket," said the author and conservationist Liz Cunningham of all that she learned from Outward Bound. (Liz's great-uncle was Outward Bound founder Kurt Hahn.) She mused:

> At first something appears impossible. But now you have this key, and you have a sense for its remarkable potential to open doors. I feel very much that I have that in common with other Outward Bounders. I meet them, and we share that powerful feeling of possibility. What could that key unlock? What could I do? It just doesn't go away.

"Uncle Kurt" urged Liz to participate in Outward Bound, and after he passed away in the mid-1970s, she attended a course in North Carolina. That experience infused her with a sense of possibility that has fueled a lifetime of passionate work in nature.

> When I got to Outward Bound, I was just so overwhelmed. I was a really scrawny kid. I was not healthy. My experience at Outward Bound was about staying precisely in the moment. I told myself, "If I can take the next step, then I'm good. I *can* take the next step." At the end I was absolutely astonished that I'd come through it.

What she discovered in herself—that magical key—lies at the heart of Expeditionary Leadership.

My Leadership Journey

In 2012 I was invited to join the leadership team of a ninety-five-year-old, fourth-generation-owned auto dealer group, despite having no experience in the auto industry. My position was called director of corporate potential, and my job was to help transform the company from a traditional business to one that would, if you pardon the pun, become a vehicle for good in the world. In the years since, the Grappone Automotive Group has become an entirely different type of business: one that puts people and relationships at the forefront of everything it does. We have received recognition for our unique approach from business leaders and social scientists such as Edward Deci, who developed some of the most groundbreaking research on human motivation.

Even though I had no experience with the industry, this organizational journey followed a pattern I had come to know well during my time at Outward Bound: leaving the comfort of the familiar and leading a group of people into the unknown. Both those around me and I had moments of doubt and uncertainty. We were challenged and tested, finding skills and strengths that we didn't know we had. We failed multiple times, and our experience was defined by what we learned and applied from those failures as much as anything else. We had to depend on each other, and in the process we discovered what we were capable of, individually and collectively. We served each other, we strived for the greater good, and we did not yield when faced with adversity. Succeeding at such an undertaking would have been impossible without my experience as a participant, instructor, and leader with Outward Bound. Even though I had earned a bachelor's in communications and a master's in business, it was my experiences at Outward Bound that taught me how to lead.

My time at Outward Bound began as a participant on a twenty-three-day mountaineering, desert hiking, and whitewater course in Utah. It then moved to leading wilderness trips in northern Minnesota and on the border in south Texas, followed by helping to manage Homeplace (the Minnesota base camp) and running a twenty-eight-day at-risk youth program.

After several years I moved to Minneapolis to open the sales department, working with corporations and schools to bring their groups to Outward Bound. After a decade I left full-time work with the Voyageur Outward Bound School and moved to Asheville, North Carolina. There, my work shifted to leading mostly professional development and team-building programs with the North Carolina Outward Bound School and, a bit later, the National Outward Bound Professional team.

Along the way I trained to become an organizational coach, enabling me to help develop some of the leadership programs that were being launched by organizations such as The Home Depot, Cox Enterprises, and Charlotte Pipe and Foundry (where I spent six years supporting organizational change efforts). I returned to school for a master's in business and entrepreneurship, where I wrote the first rough sketch of what is now this book. Over many years of working as an organizational coach and consultant, I began codifying what I had observed and the lessons I had learned. Eventually, they filled in the pieces for the framework of this book.

It has long been clear to me that people who have experience with Outward Bound have a different perspective of and approach to the world. Through Outward Bound, I found my own inner strength and resolve, and my values, compassion, and empathy. I met my wife and ultimately ended in the leadership role I now inhabit. Through Outward Bound I learned how to lead. And maybe more importantly, I learned who I am and how to contribute to my community.

I was taught, mentored, coached, and supported by great Expeditionary Leaders, and I have taught, mentored, coached, and supported those whom I have since led. You will meet some of them in the pages of this book. Some have passed away, leaving their legacy in the organizations and people whom they impacted. Others continue the Outward Bound work. They are educators and doctors and industry leaders. They are nonprofit executives and authors and social entrepreneurs. They are consultants and business coaches and yoga instructors. They are in communities across the globe. They are generally not the headline grabbers and attention seekers; in most cases they have led in anonymity. They are all Expeditionary Leaders.

There are tens of thousands of us around the world who have shared this experience in our schools, at our workplaces, or in wilderness expeditions. I would posit that Outward Bound has reached more people and had a larger positive impact on people in the world than perhaps any other organization. It's just that most of us have never examined what people have done with the lessons they learned on their journey with Outward Bound.

I am immensely grateful to Outward Bound for the lessons it taught and the values it fostered in me. As a business leader I constantly draw on these. Outward Bound helped mold the ways I learned to think and respond. It gave me a model to apply to every aspect of my life. Those simple words, "to serve, to strive, and not to yield," have been the backbone of everything I have done in my life.

It is my hope that through this book, you too will gain the tools to deal with the uncertainty and rapid change of modern life and to find the key to unlock the door to the best version of yourself and your own extraordinary impact.

CHAPTER ONE

From the Wilderness to the Workplace

Adventure isn't hanging on a rope off the side of a mountain. Adventure is an attitude that we must apply to the day-to-day obstacles of life—facing new challenges, seizing new opportunities, testing our resources against the unknown and, in the process, discovering our own unique potential.

—John Amatt, author, adventurer,
and founder of One Step Beyond Worldwide

I n a classic Outward Bound wilderness trip, a group of strangers come together to immerse themselves in nature. They create community, achieve milestones, experience peaks and valleys, and then disperse to reenter their everyday lives. Instructors and course directors typically let participants know at the end of the trip that they are just beginning their Outward Bound journey. They have become Expeditionary Leaders and must discover for themselves how they will affect the world.

Outward Bound uses the wilderness as a means to midwife new possibilities about how we can show up in the world. The experience of an Outward Bound expedition gives participants the tools for bravely facing the wild unknowns in their daily lives. A perfect example of taking the philosophies of Outward Bound into a completely different context is offered by Michael Welp, a former Outward Bound leader and the cofounder of a consulting company called White Men as Full Diversity Partners. Michael's company does transformative work around inclusion and diversity, a core value of Outward Bound. With his partner and cofounder Bill Proudman, also a former Outward Bound leader, he has moved from exploring the natural wilderness to diving deep into the metaphoric wilderness of white privilege.

"We came to the conclusion that we needed to find a way to teach white guys about diversity," said Michael, who holds a PhD in human and organizational systems development.

> There are a lot of white men in leadership, and it's not sustainable for the minority group to be teaching the majority. So we decided to take a risk and put white guys in a room for three and a half days and have them focus on themselves.
>
> What does it mean to be white and male and, for many, also heterosexual? What do we not know that we don't know? Do we have culture that others assimilate to? Do we have privilege and systemic advantage? And what is our responsibility with each other to educate our group about that?

It turned out to be a transformative and life-changing "expedition" for the white men who participated. Michael explained: "We just took out the wilderness component that pushes people to grow, and put in diversity as the messy arena that you do the leadership development and human development work in."

The skills Michael developed at Outward Bound are at the core of his $4 million business that is effecting change in the world at multiple corporate levels. But Michael says the biggest changes he sees occur *within* the people who attend the programs.

"They start off thinking we're helping other people with their issues—women and people of color—but they end up having these massive changes within themselves. They discover their culture and how to get free of it, they find the freedom to step out of it."

Just as Outward Bound did for Michael, so does his company give each individual the skills and the personal transformation to birth his or her own impact on the world.

The journey of Eduardo Balarezo also reflects how Outward Bound principles can lead to a powerful impact in the wider world. Eduardo took Outward Bound to Ecuador in 2006 and served as the group's president there for five years. A serial entrepreneur, Eduardo emigrated to the United States in 2012, launching the social retail enterprise Lonesome George & Co. to benefit the Galápagos Islands. He also launched the Academy of Agents of Change, a unique educational approach based on Outward Bound principles and social entrepreneurship.

Lonesome George began as a brand that sold T-shirts and other lifestyle apparel. Eduardo committed 10 percent of the brand's revenue to funding Outward Bound programs and leadership programs for park rangers and other workers at the Galápagos National Park.

Eduardo figured, "Since I had done this with my team, why not do this with the national park and provide them with a better understanding of teamwork, leadership, resourcefulness, and respect for others and everything I knew that came from Outward Bound?"

Lonesome George was not the only new idea to come from Eduardo's Outward Bound experience. Through the Young Presidents' Organization, Eduardo was selected to organize a Latin American Center focused on multiple bottom lines (people, profit, planet). He had close to a hundred executives from around the world come to Quito, Ecuador, and delivered a three-day program that used Outward Bound methodology. Most recently, Eduardo launched Mind Shift Impact, a transformational consulting company based on Expeditionary Leadership principles.

"These different experiences with Outward Bound made me realize how potent Outward Bound is. They gave me the courage to leap forward, to say, 'I'm going to do this. I'm going to start my social enterprise. It's going to use multiple bottom lines, and I'm just going to go for it.'"

Rue Mapp, the founder of Outdoor Afro, which connects African Americans with experiences in nature, agrees that the values she learned through Outward Bound are a huge part of her work developing African American leaders.

> It's not about how many people I can get outside who look like me, but how many leaders can we cultivate in the outdoors. It's about cultivating leaders, not getting people outside. The outdoors is just a tool.
>
> How does that leadership translate into other areas of their lives even if they don't take the outdoors on as their career? How else can those opportunities serve them and their immediate sphere of influence?
>
> In a proud moment today, we are sending off a group of eleven people who are climbing Kilimanjaro. I don't know what kind of impact it will have on their lives, but I know they will be changed forever. Just like I was changed forever through my experiences. And then when they go back into their community, through their own interests, they'll decide the types of events they want to lead.

The Birth of a Philosophy

During the beginning of the past century the world was going through extreme upheaval. The majority of human culture in the Western world was moving from an agrarian to an industrial focus. As Kurt Hahn, a young German-born Jewish educator, watched the challenges of the transition, he identified what he called the six declines: fitness, initiative, imagination, craftsmanship, self-discipline, and compassion.

In 1920, he began the Schule Schloss Salem school in Germany with the intention of countering these declines. He placed service to others and compassion at the forefront of his instruction. He believed learning should be conducted experientially—through doing—with an emphasis on serving the greater good of society.

This approach to education was quickly threatened when Hitler and the Nazis rose to power. Hahn then founded the Gordonstoun School in Scotland, based on similar principles. Its alumni include Prince Philip, the Duke of Edinburgh.

As World War II erupted, Hahn was asked to develop a training program to increase the survival rates of merchant marines whose ships were being sunk by German U-boats in the North Sea. He designed an intense experience to help individuals rapidly overcome adversity and to support and trust each other. This program became the blueprint for Outward Bound.

Thomas James, dean of the Teachers College at Columbia University, explained that "Hahn likened himself to a midwife" when creating new educational institutions. "He sparked ideas for new endeavors and then left much of the development and maintenance to others." Thomas is considered one of the most knowledgeable educators about Outward Bound and its impact in the world. A veteran of several trips himself, Thomas also uses many of Outward Bound's principles in his leadership at Columbia.

This idea of midwifery—giving individuals the skills to birth their own impact on the world and then letting go and allowing others to lead—has not only created generations of Expeditionary Leaders but also allowed Outward Bound itself to "midwife" a wide range of programs that share its guiding principles: to serve, to strive, and not to yield.

These principles, which it originally promoted through wilderness expeditions, are now experienced through a wide range of organizations, such as EL (Expeditionary Learning) Education, an offshoot of Outward Bound that focuses on taking Hahn's vision into schools and school systems, and Outward Bound Professional, which partners with companies and nonprofits to transform work environments. Regardless of the population demographic or the location of the program, Outward Bound and its offspring remained committed to Hahn's legacy of moral purpose.

Former instructors and participants like Michael, Eduardo, and Rue are the "children" of Hahn's midwifery philosophy. They demonstrate how the principles of Outward Bound can be applied in many different environments to create a better and more inclusive world. The other Expeditionary Leaders featured in this book are also the products of this unique and inspiring approach to leadership—an approach that begins with a deep commitment to service.[1]

---

1. For more biographical information, visit KurtHahn.org.

To Serve

The Master doesn't talk, he acts.
When his work is done,
the people say,
"Amazing: we did it, all by ourselves!"
   — Lao-Tzu, *Tao Te Ching*

The foundation of Outward Bound's approach is service. That foundation can be traced back to the early teaching of founder Kurt Hahn at the first school he founded, Schule Schloss Salem in Germany. When Hahn founded Outward Bound in Great Britain, all the participants were trained in sea rescue to instill that sense of service to the seafaring community.

Much has been written on servant leadership. Outward Bound is certainly not an originator of this approach. What this first section offers is a different perspective on serving. Think of it as an alignment between serving oneself, serving others in the workplace, serving the community, and answering a higher calling. Orienting ourselves to service creates a paradox. Serving first requires great humility. But in serving with humility, we actually find a sense of accomplishment, achievement, and fulfillment. It is in this sweet spot that Expeditionary Leaders find their greatest strength and resolve.

CHAPTER TWO

To Serve Others

*The best way to find yourself is
to lose yourself in the service of others.*
—Mahatma Gandhi

A rthur Blank, cofounder of The Home Depot, first got acquainted with Outward Bound in the early days of the company's founding. Marjorie Buckley, who attended one of Outward Bound's first girls' courses in Minnesota and helped found the North Carolina Outward Bound School, was an early investor in Blank's new endeavor, along with her husband. It was the Buckleys who came up with the name The Home Depot.[1]

Marjorie invited Arthur to the North Carolina Outward Bound School base camp near Table Rock Mountain in the Pisgah National Forest, and there he found a philosophy that aligned with his and his partner's call to lead through service to others.

Arthur says, "Of all the organizations I've been connected to, Outward Bound has had the most significant impact on my life.

---

1. Funny story: Arthur told me how the Buckleys were traveling to New York from their home in Pennsylvania when they thought up "Home Depot." They came upon this train depot that looked just like a home, and the name just came to them!

How do we integrate that philosophy? To serve, to strive, and not to yield is very much a part of everything we do."

After retiring, Arthur founded the AMB Group, which is best known for ownership of the Atlanta Falcons and the professional soccer team Atlanta United. In addition, the group manages guest ranches in Montana, PGA Tour Superstores, and the Arthur M. Blank Family Foundation.

> I'll be 76 the end of this month. Bernie [the cofounder] will be 90. When you get to my age, you realize that one of the great things you can do in this world is be of service to others. Sometimes you can do it at work, sometimes with philanthropy. We've been able to couple it; we've been able to translate that [value] into all the existing businesses we have today: the football team, the soccer team, the golf business, our two guest ranches, our foundation. They are all built on the same principles of being of service to others.

Regardless of the focus of the endeavor or the product or service of an organization, Expeditionary Leaders like Arthur know that they are ultimately responsible for the well-being of other people—those they lead, those they encounter—and for the web of relationships that flow from their center. It is an awesome and humbling responsibility.

"I've been blessed financially. It's my opportunity and responsibility to make a difference in other people's lives in every way that I can," Arthur continued.

> A large part of my work now is the foundation, but [the "of service" atmosphere] is the essence of all of our businesses. It's always about making people happy in their lives. We focus on fans for the football team and the soccer matches, guests at the ranches. We have to do other things correctly—we have to ride

horses correctly, we have to sell food correctly. There are other fundamental skills that go with it, but the underlying essence is making sure people are happy. That's being of service to them.

Bringing Purpose to Work

Modern engagement theory has identified a sense of purpose as being critical to people's intrinsic motivation. Intrinsically motivated employees work harder, produce more, stay longer, and live healthier lives than those who are motivated through external circumstances. In fact, purpose has been cited by numerous business authors and researchers as an integral part of creating a successful organization.

Crafting purpose comes from a leader's own value system. Expeditionary Leaders understand this and make it central to the focus of the organizations they lead. Outward Bound has lived in the space of deep, meaningful purpose for more than half a century.

Arthur Blank and Bernie Marcus were dialed in to this focus long before social scientists and authors put a name to it; they used this deep sense of purpose to build The Home Depot and revolutionize the entire home improvement industry. "One of the awards I am most proud of we received in 2000, the year I got ready to retire," said Arthur.

> In that year, Home Depot was ranked first in social responsibility by the Harris Interactive Survey. At the same time, company stock was up 45 percent for the year, earnings 48 percent, and sales climbed 47 percent.
>
> It shows you can serve both masters. Many people believe that if you focus on making money, you can't focus on doing good in the world. The truth of the matter is that we need to give work purpose beyond just financial. Doing good work and

driving the right kind of behavior in business, like people serving others, can produce good financial results. It creates the right kind of chemistry and stimulus for the people we are serving, and then we have the opportunity to take that success and reinvest it back in the community.

Do You Go to Work or to Mission?

"This concept of service that [Outward Bound founder] Kurt Hahn felt was so important," said Laura Kohler, senior vice president of human resources, stewardship, and sustainability for Kohler Co. "Outward Bound is purposeful. It builds leaders for the future. It builds character in people." This is also what Laura is doing at Kohler: creating a common sense of "why we are here" that attracts people who, like herself, feel called to lead the change toward greater sustainability.

Laura's first experience with Outward Bound was as a teenager on a mountaineering course with the Pacific Crest Outward Bound School. She returned to Outward Bound as an instructor for Voyageur Outward Bound School's Chicago urban programs, as well as as a wilderness instructor for the Voyageur school in Montana. Laura has since joined the board of Outward Bound USA and served as its chair, becoming one of the first former instructors to help guide the federation of schools.

"At Kohler people don't come to make a beautiful faucet or toilet. They're here because they want to give back and make the world a better place. They want to be a part of a company that is an additive," Laura said

As an Expeditionary Leader, Laura helps guide thousands of Kohler associates who put the value of community responsibility into action with projects such as bringing safe drinking water to impoverished locations where employees live and work. Product designers and engineers worked on creating a filtration system that was affordable and easily transportable. Packaging designers developed a six-sided box that allowed them to ship nine filtration systems in a container versus six in a square box, further reducing the costs of production. Kohler's multicultural team of associates even considered the color of the filtration system to avoid offending any culture. This project was born out of a workshop created by Kohler called "Innovation for Good," which provides associates with the opportunity to harness their individual skills and collective knowledge to make the world a better place.

It makes sense that a company that produces faucets and toilets might also tackle the problem of creating a safe delivery mechanism for potable water. But to use its collective skills and knowledge, an Expeditionary Leader needed to be called. Laura explained:

> We activate our associates to develop and adapt their knowledge. How we can create products that are sustainable? How can we lower the footprint on water usage? How do we make Kohler a net positive company? How do we make Kohler a legacy company that people in a hundred years will say, "There was this company that actually did good. It sold stuff, but it actually made the world a better place, strengthened the communities where it worked. It actually cleaned the environment. It contributed so that everybody could have access to clean water." I want to be that company.

• • •

I observed this power of mission-driven servant leadership multiple times during my career. When I began working with The Home Depot through the North Carolina Outward Bound School, I heard countless stories from store managers about their encounters with

Arthur Blank and Bernie Marcus. They would recall coming down an aisle and discovering one of them straightening a display or speaking with a customer. Respect for the founders' commitment to service ran deep.

Perhaps the best example I saw was with Charlotte Pipe & Foundry. Outward Bound brought me in to help develop a leadership program with the company's third-generation family leaders. Cousins Frank Dowd IV and Roddy Dowd Jr. took over leadership from their fathers. Both men had recognized that global markets were opening and posed a risk to the company. They decided to develop their leadership bench by pushing decision-making down and across the company. This new structure meant that people unaccustomed to making strategic company decisions were now being asked to step up and take on leadership roles.

Changing a century-old company is not an easy undertaking.[2] It would have been nearly impossible if not for the deep respect the two cousins had earned through service to their employees.

One story that stands out for me came from some of the foundry managers. They told me how Roddy would show up on the hottest days of the summer, put on work clothes, and work part of the foundry workers' shift. This simple act of kindness was an extension of the deep-held respect that the leadership of Charlotte Pipe extended to all its workers and vendors, and even to me when I visited their offices to train or coach. In turn, the employees honored the Dowd family through decades of their own service to the company. Many have worked there for their entire careers. Frank and Roddy exemplified the qualities that underpin the Expeditionary Leadership ideal of service. It was a privilege to work with men of such great character.

---

2. I would rediscover this when I joined the leadership team of The Grappone Automotive Group in 2012.

REFLECTION

1. Which story or stories in the chapter most resonate with you and why?

2. How have you been in service to others in your life? How did that affect your own life and who you are today?

3. Where in your current life are you in service to others? In what ways could you take it further?

4. What is one area in which your gifts and talents could make a positive difference right now? What could you do? What is one step you can take toward contributing? When will you do it?

CHAPTER THREE

To Serve a Higher Calling

Becoming a leader is synonymous with becoming yourself.
It is precisely that simple and it is also that difficult.
—Warren Bennis

Expeditionary Leaders are rarely content with what is. They are called to lead the change to make things better, whether that means creating new movements, serving in public office, or making long-standing organizations better corporate citizens.

Laura Kohler answered her call to lead when she helped put her family's 136-year-old business on a path to a greater purpose. As the senior vice president of human resources, stewardship, and sustainability at Kohler Co., Laura guides three hundred human resource associates around the globe. They are responsible for harnessing the human energy of more than thirty-five thousand employees not only in their work directly for the company, but also in service of its public-service goals. In fact, Kohler has set a goal to be a net-zero company in greenhouse gas emissions and landfill waste by 2035. Laura believes that this ambitious goal can be met only by tapping into the deep motivations of her team and encouraging them to answer their own calls to lead.

"We are deploying our associates all over the world to do things, whether it is to plant trees, or build a library, or tutor. We tell our associates, 'If you have a good idea that helps your community, we'll put some money into it and you can go make a difference.'"

A few months after joining the Grappone Automotive Group in 2012, I launched an "Expeditionary Leadership journey" that helped the company's leaders to find their own service calling. The leadership team gathered on a Sunday morning in March when the dealerships were closed and spent several hours completing a series of problem-solving challenges that I designed. Many of the managers had been with the company more than twenty years, and yet for the most part, they worked in separate divisions and departments. Grappone at the time was a holding company with individual franchises. Employees identified more with their franchise and their department than they did with the company.

At the end of the day I asked them to consider what being a part of this company meant to them. We filled a wall with adjectives and began a process of finding common ground, paring down the dozens of words into categories from which I led a series of discussions. After several sessions we ended up with the mission of the Grappone Automotive Group: "Dedication to building lifelong relationships with our team members, guests, and community by serving with integrity, kindness, and respect."

Those words emerged organically from the team members who had dedicated much of their lives to the company. Once the mission was articulated, the culture began to rapidly coalesce around it. What emerged was a notion of "One Grappone." The company has attracted new team members who would have never considered working in car sales but who are drawn to the notion of serving people and transforming an industry. In addition, that clear sense of service to a greater good has led to other significant changes—everything from a transparent pricing model to product specialists (those in sales roles) who work commission-free and are rewarded for making a difference in the lives of the company's customers.

Paving the Way for Those Who Follow

Sometimes the calling is unexpected. Leaders must be prepared to take risks and pursue unexplored paths, paving the way for those who follow. This ability to lead into the unknown is a singularly important entrepreneurial skill that Expeditionary Leaders lean into. It is how Outdoor Afro, a nonprofit that connects African American leaders with nature through outdoor experiences, came to be.

"I was about to go to grad school and get an MBA when my mentor asked me, 'What would I want to do if time and money were not an issue?'" said Rue Mapp, the founder of Outdoor Afro. "I just opened my mouth and my life fell out. I said I would probably start a website to reconnect African Americans to the outdoors. We both took a moment, a beat, to figure out what I just said and how that connected to anything we were working on at the time."

Rue realized that what she had just verbalized was the coming together of all the parts of who she was and what she loved: digital technology, the outdoors, and community-building communications. "It was really my truth."

Rue discovered her passion for the outdoors and risk-taking in part from her Outward Bound expedition in the southern High Sierra in California. When the call to lead into the unknown came, Rue was willing to listen. Her previous Outward Bound experience played a big part in giving her the confidence to pursue her vision and light a path for the thousands who would soon follow. In fact, Rue's Outward Bound experience has become part of her organization's creation story, which she shares with groups across the United States.

In 2009, Rue launched Outdoor Afro with a blog that included a picture of herself on the side of a mountain on her Outward Bound course. Today Outdoor Afro is a national 501(c)(3) organization with offices in Oakland and Washington, D.C. Outdoor Afro has networks north of thirty-two thousand people in thirty states and has trained eighty people to be leaders in their communities.

Following the Path as It Unfolds

Expeditionary Leaders are open to an outcome whatever it may be. They follow a path as it unfolds. For example, Michael Welp, a former Outward Bound leader and cofounder of the consulting company White Men as Full Diversity Partners, didn't know where his curiosity about diversity issues would lead him. His interest developed in graduate school at American University in Washington, D.C. After grad school, his work for Outward Bound took him to Lesotho, South Africa, where he led Outward Bound courses that integrated black and white South Africans for the first time. Something as simple as two men of different races sharing a beer together after a day of team building had never been done before. The experience opened Michael's eyes in a way that would lead to his life's work.

> I saw how white guys were demonized as oppressors, and yet one on one, they were good guys—they're just like me. I realized I needed to go work with my group—with white guys—because that is what is needed in the world. Why should women and people of color have to carry the burden of helping us see our privilege?
>
> The white men I met in Lesotho were all really good guys, but they were part of an oppressive system. There was no good place for white men to learn about diversity. Often [diversity training] is set up as a mixed group, and often they end up being blamed. We needed a safe place where we can work through our learning with each other. That launched my career.

Michael returned to the States committed to answering this call to lead white men into the unknown space of acknowledging their privilege and using it for good. Since 1997, he has been showing white men how they can help create a more inclusive and diverse workplace.

The Call to Service

Expeditionary Leaders are problem solvers; the desire to solve the world's problems is often what sparks that call to lead. Take Maggie Fox, one of the first female instructors at Outward Bound. Maggie left Outward Bound to go to law school in order to follow her passion of protecting the environment.

"Most people go to law school to be a lawyer," said Maggie. "I didn't. I wanted to be an advocate, and in my mind being an advocate meant understanding the law." Maggie's career led her to the Sierra Club, where she worked for twenty years and eventually became deputy executive director. She reflected:

> The Sierra Club was the only environmental organization in the entire progressive movement that understood the power and the need to build relationships across the broad progressive infrastructure, not just the environmental organizations. Up until then everybody in the environmental movement spent all their time with each other, coalition building only with other environmental groups, which always felt incredibly limiting to me.
>
> There was a big moment happening, and we knew we needed to get on the front end of this. We needed to build relationships with the women's movement. We had to build relationships with civic society organizations. We had to build relationships with all of the progressive-movement infrastructure.

At the Sierra Club, Maggie was able to do this important work of connecting various progressive nonprofits. Little did she know that an event was soon to occur that would change the landscape of the progressive movement and her career. The skills she had been mastering and the relationships she had been building in the Sierra Club would come into play when a call to an even greater purpose struck.

In 2000, the infamous US presidential race between Al Gore and George W. Bush led to some soul-searching within progressive organizations who were greatly disappointed when Bush won despite Gore's winning the popular vote.

"After that race we progressive leaders realized that we were unprepared for the coordinated work that was happening on the other side. We actually had to figure out how to work together to be more effective," Maggie said. As a result, Cecile Richards founded America Votes, whose stated goal is "to build a year-round coalition that makes the progressive community stronger."

In 2005, Richards called on Maggie to take over leadership of the organization. Maggie answered that call with a resounding yes. The election of 2000 was the trigger that opened Maggie to the idea of leaving the comfort of her known career to create an even larger impact in the world.

As national president, Maggie was tasked with coordinating the political efforts of seventeen organizations working with America Votes. When she left in 2007, it had grown to thirty-seven organizations.[1] Under Maggie, America Votes was credited with playing an instrumental role in the higher voter turnout experienced by the Democratic Party in the 2006 and 2008 elections and contributing to the election of Barack Obama as president of the United States. "I loved it," Maggie said.

> I loved bringing those people together. I loved serving them. Showing them ways that they could be stronger. Showing that little tiny groups could be stronger by working with groups that had

---

1. Maggie left the organization when her husband, Mark Udall, declared his candidacy for the United States Senate and her work became a conflict of interest.

long history in elections. How big groups could learn a lot from these smaller groups that were fresh and new and reaching people in different ways.

• • •

All Expeditionary Leaders are mission driven. It starts at the core of their being and spreads through their work. They recognize the importance of their impact from the start. "The important thing is to combine what you love to do with serving the world—that's where your greatest power is. If you connect your greatest passions with the world's needs, that takes you on a path filled with purpose and what seems impossible, might just be possible," said Liz Cunningham, writer and conservationist. That is what Expeditionary Leaders are called to do—for themselves and for those they lead.

REFLECTION

1. Which story or stories in the chapter most resonate with you and why?

2. In what areas of your life have you answered a call to serve something greater? How has that affected your life and who you have become?

3. In what areas do you now feel "called"? Are you answering that calling? Why or why not?

4. What's one thing you could do right now to align your current work and life with a greater calling? Who can help guide you along the path of service?

5. When you look at the world, what gnaws at you? If you were not limited by time or money, where would you put your energy? What is one step you can take to begin working on this issue?

CHAPTER FOUR

To Serve a Community

Life's most persistent and urgent question is:
What are you doing for others?
　　—Martin Luther King Jr.

O
utward Bound has led people deep into wilderness settings, up mountains, out on the seas, and on ropes courses in the United States since the early 1960s with very few accidents. Hanging on a rope on the side of a cliff sixty feet above the ground can seem fraught with danger. But the reality is, those events are thoroughly vetted, and the staff is trained to manage the risks. Systems have built-in safety redundancies, and Outward Bound leaders are mentored, trained, and promoted based on their ability to safely manage risk. The vast majority of accidents that do happen are minor. They rarely involve things such as rock climbing or whitewater paddling and are more likely the result of a twisted ankle on a portage trail. They are preventable by something as simple as making sure participants have had enough food and water.

Expeditionary Leaders always put the safety of the team at the forefront of their mind. But what Outward Bound has long recognized is that the social experience of the expedition is the place of greatest exposure to participants and that the highest risks are emotional. And so it is here that Expeditionary Leaders put their greatest focus: in building a safe community to enable participants to mentally step out on a limb and into the unknown.

Modeling Vulnerability

Expeditionary Leaders proactively foster a sense of belonging and inclusion in a team, which allows individuals to take greater physical and emotional risks while dealing with uncertainty. Building that community of safety and trust is critical to the success of the venture, whether it is an outdoor expedition, the launch of a new product, or a company pivot.

Creating an atmosphere of safety and trust is a deliberate and multistep process. The first step requires the leader to model what they expect. For example, groups on Outward Bound expeditions spend a lot of time in circles to emphasize that leaders are equal members in the circle, not separate from it. In the same way, Michael Welp of White Men as Full Diversity Partners creates safe places for people to share by sharing himself. His organization operates multiday experiences called caucuses, where white men learn how to create more inclusivity in their work and personal lives. He noted:

> One of the things we learned early on is that you can't be the neutral facilitator and not share your stuff—because the participants will just tune out and become observers. We have to talk about our lives and what we're learning about diversity and our own blind spots. We model being on that continuous journey, just like we want them to be.

Leaving Your Ego behind

Stepping up as an Expeditionary Leader requires a deep awareness of self and a willingness to share all the parts of yourself—warts and all. That means parking your ego at the door.

Bill Proudman, cofounder of White Men as Full Diversity Partners, showed his "warts" by inviting his father to some of the first caucuses that he and Michael led. "That brought [Bill's] own stuff into the room," recounted Michael. "He demonstrated taking emotional risks." This vulnerability and lack of ego encouraged the participants to also bring their "stuff" regarding diversity and inclusion into the room.

Expeditionary Leaders practice humility, acknowledging that they don't know all the answers and that their job is to facilitate learning for others and for themselves. They are comfortable meeting participants where they are, which can include being challenged.

"We allow participants to voice their concerns, their frustrations about being there, and I validate wherever people are at," Michael said. "My perspective is never that another person's opinion is wrong. It's most likely only incomplete, and my responsibility is to help the person keep working on broadening it."

One participant opened a caucus by saying, "This is a worthless waste of our company's money. We're not going to learn anything here." Michael gave a heart-centered response, thanking him for making it safer for everyone in the room to say what they were really thinking and feeling.

"I validated his skepticism. He became a really engaged participant after that for the rest of the caucus. We have to always accept people where they are."

Building Community

Some might think that Outward Bound would perpetuate the American archetype of the "rugged individualist." But nothing could be further from the truth. Expeditionary Leaders are at their core connectors. They understand that the greatest learning occurs not in isolation but in community. Only in a strong community can individuals take the risks that allow deep, lasting growth.

Regardless of the plan for the organization and the goals that measure its success, Expeditionary Leaders understand that fostering connections is crucial to long-lasting impact. The social psychologists Edward Deci and Richard Ryan refer to this as *relatedness*: our deep need to be connected and to have compassion and care for others. When connections are deepened and people find commonality, individual values begin to better align with those of the community.

For Michael of White Men as Full Diversity Partners, fostering connections in the prickly arena of diversity and inclusion has been key to his organization's success.

> It's that sense of allowing people to slow down, to come together, to really hear each other and feel their impact, so they get a visceral experience of what partnership looks like in a way they have never experienced before. They have to get an experience of what we're trying to create in the world in order to carry that forward.

Expeditionary Leaders focus on and wait for these moments of slowing down and coming together in order to build trust and create the safe spaces people need to venture into the unknown.

Building community leads to a much stronger organization. Too often we succumb to the cult of the personality of the leader. But becoming too dependent on an individual leader puts an organization at risk. This is why Expeditionary Leaders strive to cultivate both independence *and* interdependence. They build a web of strengths and trusting relationships that maximize the strength of the individuals.

The interdependent community that Maggie Fox and her team built in her time leading the progressive organization America Votes was one of her proudest achievements:

> We had my last board meeting and the people stood up and gave me an ovation, which I didn't think I deserved. I remember standing there, and thinking to myself, *How can I respond?* Standing there didn't feel right.
>
> So I dropped into a deep curtsy. I bowed to them. And I remembered thinking to myself, *This is exactly how I feel. I know to do this because I know that as your leader I trusted you and you gave me back trust. And we moved.* We were on a rope together, and we moved. To me, this exemplified what I felt they had given me. They were honoring me, but my response was, *No, this is completely a two-way street.*

As an Outward Bound instructor and facilitator, I was trained to focus on group dynamics. Expeditionary Leadership requires the leader to balance attention between the individual members of the group, the group dynamics, and the ultimate performance of the team. Too much attention on any corner of this triangle, and the development of the team will stall.

For the first year of the organizational change at Grappone, we met in monthly leadership "pods." The groups were cross-functional and blended corporate and individual-franchise leaders. We shared insights as we learned about organizations known for great cultures. The members of each group also selected projects to tackle that helped the company implement its strategic plan and achieve its vision.

During this year much of my focus was on the relationships between participants. We launched a formal coaching program, and I met with each member on a monthly basis. Monthly group meetings included relationship-building activities and projects requiring collaboration between managers who had never worked together before.

The greatest result of this year was fostering a sense of community among stores and departments. When I joined Grappone, it was a holding company that operated several separate retail operations and a wholesale parts operation. Just as I had experienced at Charlotte Pipe, the silos of the departments and divisions dissolved through a deliberate focus on building community within the company. People now take it for granted that a product specialist can travel store to store with a guest and be welcomed and supported regardless of which store she walks into. That wouldn't have even been considered just a few years prior.

$$\bullet \ \bullet \ \bullet$$

Without a circle of safety and trust, we are just individuals plodding along our own paths, missing out on the beauty and energy that come with living in community and working on common goals. The power of the collective can be harnessed only when we trust each other enough to share the load. As Maggie Fox explains:

"*We* are going to do this together. We all *need* to do this together. We can't pull this off if we don't step off together."

REFLECTION

1. Which story or stories in the chapter most resonate with you and why?

2. Where in your life have you been drawn to build community? How has that affected your life? How has it made you who you are?

3. Where in your life are you currently helping to build community?

4. What's one thing you could do right now to help build community where you live and work?

5. Where are you most needed? What is one step you can take to build relationships with those people in need? What more can you do?

CHAPTER FIVE

To Serve the Learning Experience

Learning is finding out what you already know.
Doing is demonstrating that you know it. Teaching
is reminding others that they know just as well as you.
We are all learners, doers, and teachers.
　　—Richard Bach

Imagine a group of strangers coming together and embarking on a wilderness expedition with little to no experience in the outdoors. Within a matter of a few days they will be expected to lead their own expedition with little support from their guides. That is the experiential learning model that Outward Bound has perfected since it was brought to the United States in the early 1960s.

This highly effective teaching method requires a rapid transfer of *knowledge and responsibility* and results in a high degree of *autonomy and mastery* in its participants—two components that social scientists know are critical in developing intrinsic motivation and discretionary effort in people. Expeditionary Leaders are expert educators. They understand that experience, inspiration, and engagement are the most effective methods of imparting learning.

Laura Kohler, vice president of Kohler Co.'s HR function, bakes experiential learning into the philosophy of the company:

We follow the 70-20-10 model. Seventy percent of learning happens through your experiences, 20 percent is coaching from a mentor or manager, and 10 percent is formal training.

We really try to load our high-potential people up with great experiences first and foremost. What's in that 70 percent? It's more than your day-to-day job. It's an extra team, a task force, a short-term assignment, a non-home-country assignment. Something that gets them uncomfortable and pushes them. That's where the learning happens.

Finding the Teachable Moment

As Laura alluded to, experiential learning involves moving out of your comfort zone. It means that you don't know what you're going to learn from the experience until the moment presents itself. It requires leaders and participants to stay focused on the evolving dynamics of a situation in order to find those teachable moments.

Luis Benitez, a world-renowned mountain guide who has summited Everest six times, captured the essence of leading into those moments:

> As an Expeditionary Leader you are accustomed to leading into the unknown. Every time you head out, you don't know what is going to happen. Outward Bound gives you the humility to know and learn that you don't have all the answers, that you're all in it together, and your biggest job is to pull out all of the strengths and lessons for others. Be the conductor of that orchestra, and bring those things to bear.

Luis began working for the Colorado Outward Bound School as a teenager, eventually facilitating leadership- and team-building programs with Outward Bound's corporate branch, Outward Bound Professional. His path eventually took him to Vail Resorts, where he built an experiential development model based on Outward Bound's principles. In 2015 he was hired as the first director of Colorado's Outdoor Recreation Industry Office.

Expeditionary Leaders depend on two techniques to advance learning: The first involves taking advantage of teachable moments. Leaders may appear to be doing nothing during vast parts of the expedition, but they are actually intently watching and waiting. Listening to conversations and watching interactions, they are waiting for those moments when they can help make a connection that sparks an insight and activates learning. The art of Expeditionary Leadership is in recognizing these moments and catalyzing the connections they present.

The second tool is the debriefing, used to help participants identify and reflect on what they have learned. As opposed to most organizations where little time is spent reflectively, Outward Bound expeditions require numerous debriefings—sometimes at the end of an experience or event, and often at the end of a day. This reflective time is critical to both individual and collective learning. It allows the participants to step out of the experience and deepen the connections that were made during those teachable moments. The debriefing also serves as a platform for transferring the knowledge to the next activity, project, or day.

Laura Kohler explained how coaches who are trained in debriefing are important to Kohler's employee-development process. Coaches help employees to pause and reflect on an experience. They ask powerful questions, then listen and reframe the answers to help participants deepen their learning from a teachable moment. This process allows Laura's team to champion learning across the organization.

Michael Welp's work around diversity also depends heavily upon debriefings and reflection exercises to develop a more inclusive workforce and society. "My workshop participants are a little thrown off when they come in a room and they have twenty chairs in a circle in a room with no tables, and flip charts around the room with no PowerPoint," said Michael, the founder of White Men as Full Diversity Partners.

> But after the completion of a program, many men say they thought and reflected more in the last four days than they have in their entire lives.
>
> That's so similar to what happens on an Outward Bound course: We give them compelling experiences and ask them to reflect on them. We are there to support them and challenge them from a place of love. We are connecting with them and having compassion for them and modeling the compassion that we want them to have with each other.

Letting Go

As team members grow in their capacity, the role of the Expeditionary Leader shifts. At the beginning of an expedition, leaders are pure teachers. Skill acquisition, both technical and interpersonal, is the main focal point. But the biggest impact of experiential learning comes when the teacher lets go, giving the team the space to fail or succeed on its own.

"You start out teaching. You get to a point where the team is moving beyond you," said Laura Kohler. "Strong leaders build strong teams whose members grow to operate independently." This is the real goal of an Expeditionary Leader. Success happens when the team no longer needs its leader.

Here's how Rue Mapp of Outdoor Afro explained the letting-go process. When we spoke, she had just witnessed members of her leadership volunteer team heading to Africa to climb Mount Kilimanjaro in Tanzania—without her:

> The people have developed their own expedition community amongst themselves. For me to go to Kilimanjaro with them

would be disruptive of that. That would be a grave miscarriage of my leadership, to parachute in on their experience.

They as a group will define what success looks like, and they will achieve it.

In June 2018 five members of her team found success at the top of the 19,341-foot summit. Rue's approach reflects again that philosophy of midwifery—giving individuals the skills to birth their own impact on the world and then letting go and allowing others to lead.

Leading Leaders

Outward Bound wilderness expeditions follow a pattern. During the beginning of the expedition, referred to as *immersion and training,* two leaders teach everything from campcraft and navigation to running debriefing and conflict-resolution sessions. In the second part, called *the main expedition,* the Outward Bound leaders are more like guides—waiting for teachable moments, coaching the day's leaders on running their own debriefings, and stepping in only when necessary to continue the learning progression. The two Outward Bound leaders constantly monitor the group and discuss its progress with each other. During the final stage, the group operates autonomously, and the Outward Bound leaders simply shadow it as a safety net. This is the expeditionary learning model.

During my years working with Charlotte Pipe and Foundry, I saw this pattern on micro and macro levels. Each year a group of high-potential leaders came on a wilderness trip in the mountains of North Carolina, where they learned the Expeditionary Leadership model. This was followed by a year of development during which they worked on strategic projects for the company and continued their growth as leaders. I led classroom training sessions and offered one-on-one coaching for several of these groups.

Many of those managers were then called on to lead the organizational change of Charlotte Pipe. When the company decided to purchase another, smaller company for the first time in its century-long history, one of these participants asked to lead the merger. Exposing more managers to the Expeditionary Leadership model allowed Charlotte Pipe to reach for leadership downward and outward throughout the company's divisions. The result was a remarkable evolution that helped Charlotte Pipe remain resilient and agile as international markets opened up and competition grew fiercer.

Charlotte Pipe evolved by deepening the learning of its managers. The leadership didn't necessarily know what was coming, but they built their bench by serving the learning of their greatest asset, the employees. When the need arrived, they had a bench of young leaders ready to answer the call.

Peter Bailey also uses these Outward Bound ideals of teaching, letting go, and leading leaders in his work at the Prouty Project, a strategic planning and leadership development firm based in Minneapolis. He was one of the first Outward Bound urban instructors in the country and went on to launch some of the first educational reform programs using Outward Bound principles in the classroom through the Voyageur Outward Bound School. "Leading for legacy is the highest end for leadership," he said.

> How do we pass this on? How do I bring someone younger than me, or at a lower level than me, to take on what I can do?
>
> I think of us building a ladder of leading self, leading others, and leading the business. I call it L3. If you're going to start a learning journey with us, you need to go through the L3 process. We're engaging people and inciting them to contribute in a whole new way. They're now becoming those lighthouses of leadership that others are drawn to.

• • •

Whether as leaders managing a project, a department, or a classroom, most of us have been taught to define the scope of a focus area—a project, or a department with a budget and goals, or a classroom of students with expected learning outcomes. We plan around those goals, manage to them, and track and measure the results. We analyze the performance, look for the learning, and then determine the next set of goals and assumptions. Our success as leaders tends to be measured by how well we meet these goals.

But from its inception, Outward Bound founder Kurt Hahn had different ideas about education and leadership. For him, the journey was not the path to some destination. *The journey was the destination. The experience was the education.* Creating the journey and then allowing participants to take responsibility for their own growth are the key to success.

REFLECTION

1. Which story or stories in the chapter most resonate with you and why?

2. Have you directly experienced any great models of leadership? What about those leaders made them great?

3. Where in your life have you experienced the greatest growth and learning? How has that affected your own leadership?

4. What is one area in your life where learning and growth would make the biggest impact right now?

5. Who can help support you in taking this "leader as learner" journey? Who is your champion?

To Strive

None of us, I suspect, who was not an outdoorswoman before all this has become an outdoorswoman because of it, but that was never the point; in fact, whichever of us liked it the least has probably come off best, having learned more than any of us what she is capable of, and that is the point. We are better than we know. If we can be made to see it, then perhaps for the rest of our lives we will be unwilling to settle for less.

—Barbara LaFontaine, a student in the
first women's Outward Bound course

This section reflects a distinguishing aspect of becoming an Expeditionary Leader. When one leaves the safety of the harbor and ventures outward bound, the journey will inevitably present challenges. The Expeditionary Leader uses this uncertainty, adversity, and challenge as a platform for personal development. Stepping into the unknown ultimately teaches us about ourselves. It is important to note that Outward Bound itself was born during a time of extreme world upheaval.

Risk is inherent in any endeavor, and striving involves a willingness to fail. Striving is about continuing to push onward when most others would quit. It requires us to take each setback as a learning opportunity and quickly apply that learning to the next situation. Striving is when we find out who we are.

CHAPTER SIX

To Strive through Uncertainty

I don't want to be the guy who has the answer.
I want to be a part of the systems of solution build-
ing, collaborative learning, team wisdom, and how
we set up the conditions for those to happen.
　—Peter Bailey, Prouty Project

Y ou might imagine the leader of wilderness expeditions as an expert who drills his people with push-ups and lectures them
about the right way to do things, but with Expeditionary
Leaders, nothing could be further from the truth. In an Outward
Bound expedition, the leader has as much to learn as the students.

Don't get me wrong. Outward Bound doesn't believe in depart-
ing on an expedition without thorough training and planning for
the leader as well as for the team. But this training and planning
look different from traditional training. Before they set out, the team
puts in a great deal of work to build norms and values, set expecta-
tions, and establish who is responsible for each aspect of learning.
But rather than lead the team down an imposed path, the leader
invites the group to set these norms. They find their way together,
with each person learning and growing on their own journey.

Learning While Leading

Paul "Pablo" Stayton has the heart and soul of a true Expeditionary Leader. He knows that the growth of the leader happens simultaneously with the growth of the people he or she is leading. Pablo was molded as an educator and Expeditionary Leader during his decade-long tenure at the Voyageur Outward Bound school, leading wilderness trips along the United States' southern border and deep into the Copper Canyon in Mexico. Later on, as the dean of faculty and a humanities educator at the private Watershed School in Boulder, he was charged with leading a group of students to China and building a curriculum on Chinese history, culture, and language—without having any background in the subject. His Outward Bound experience in immersing students—and himself—into completely unfamiliar situations became the model for his journey to China. He recalled:

> I had to engage my students for three straight hours every day for a whole semester in Chinese history, which I knew nothing about. Most educators would dread that. But to me, it was like, Oh my god, I wish I had four hours, because there are so many possibilities. It was an adventure into the unknown for me. It was an adventure into the unknown for my students.

Pablo gave each student in his class a Chinese dynasty to study. They spent three hours a day for a week and a half learning all they could discover about their dynasty. It was up to each student to determine what was important to know about their dynasty and to prepare some type of visual presentation. At the end, the students had created a visual timeline of five thousand years of Chinese history. Pablo didn't know what the next step would be. He was opening himself to the joy of learning along with his students. He explained:

> The different Chinese belief systems started to emerge and solidify over time—Confucianism, and Taoism, and Buddhism, and

Legalism. It actually explained how something like Tiananmen Square could happen and be accepted by the majority of the Chinese population. We started to see these threads, and as the kids made these connections and I made these connections, we became more and more excited.

This approach to teaching—allowing leaders to follow a thread and learn as they lead—is a vast departure from the approach taken in the majority of our current institutions. Professionals spend years becoming subject matter experts, mastering the information, knowledge, and ability to bring their expertise to whatever organization they are seeking to lead. Business plans are judged first and foremost on the strength of the founders' background. Advanced positions often require advanced degrees and previous experience. Yet here we have the story of an educator who had spent the majority of his career teaching classes about Mexico creating a powerful educational experience about China, leading his students by being a learner alongside them.

Pablo had no idea where the subject matter would lead him or his students. He gave himself and his students the space to find what interested them and to learn from it.

Equally important, he trusted both his students and the process. He guided them to learn. He didn't dictate what they should learn or how they should learn it. From this deep trust, his students learned well beyond what we would even think was possible in a typical classroom scenario.

This classroom model was actually only the first step of a uniquely immersive learning experience, Pablo said.

We got into all of these concepts and all these ideas, and to make it real we went to San Francisco and actually stayed just outside Chinatown. We spent six or seven days in Chinatown interviewing people. We found this youth organization of first-generation Chinese who were all high school students. Our students spent a day and a half with these youth and working with elders in the community. The elders only spoke Cantonese, with the youth translating for our kids. It was this immersion into Chinese culture in Chinatown, San Francisco.

We're staying at this youth hostel outside Chinatown, which is so international. There are so many languages, and all these people from all over the world staying there. It just increases the sense of adventure, and importance, and amazement to what the world has to offer.

Pablo, as the Expeditionary Leader, had no idea what subject matters would be broached. It was impossible to predict what interactions or insights would occur. And so, he relinquished much of the day-to-day leadership to his students, while being ready to help them make connections between their interests and the material.

When I worked for the Grappone Automotive Group, I had my own corporate experience leading through uncertainty. In 2013, the company decided to make a radical shift in its selling model. We determined that the traditional way of selling cars was not in alignment with our values and mission, and so we brought in a consulting group who had helped dealer groups like ours. After assessing our leadership team, the consultant felt we had the right leadership in place to make the leap to a completely different type of selling model.

We gathered to decide whether or not to move into this unknown world. The consultant told us that if we said yes, we should expect that the next twelve months would be the most challenging time of our careers, that we would lose the majority of our sales team and have to rebuild with new and different types of people, and that the change would cost tens of thousands of dollars in lost revenue.

This was our "burn the lifeboats" moment. After nearly ninety years in business we decided to take the company into a completely uncharted direction. Soon after we took that leap, the consultant's words proved true. We found ourselves in new territory, with no map to guide us and very few dealer groups like us out there in the world from which to learn. Over the coming months and years the entire leadership team learned how to dig in, discover new solutions, listen to our teams, and trust one another. The national recognition that we eventually received only came because we were willing to embrace the uncertainty of a completely unknown path.

Curiosity as a Leadership Skill

Former US senator Mark Udall has been the executive director of the Colorado Outward Bound School. Reflecting on his time in government service, he homed in on the importance of being curious and open to learning.

> There were two areas in which I really loved being a senator. Number one was inspiring young people to get involved with public service, to know they can make a difference, which is part of the Outward Bound ethos. The other thing was more personal. I got to be curious. Any day of the week, if I became interested in a subject—because it has an effect on our lives, on our country's standing, or our economy or whatever—the smartest, most brilliant people in the country in any vocation would be willing to come sit down with me and educate me.
>
> Being curious and being open to learning is really what life's about. You have to be humble, you have to be willing to be embarrassed, and chided, and to feel like you don't know anything. I loved that part of the job. On behalf of over six million Coloradans I could put my curiosity and my interest in learning to work on their behalf.

REFLECTION

1. Which story or stories in the chapter most resonate with you and why?

2. What uncertainty are you currently facing in your life or work? What is it teaching you about yourself?

3. What opportunities might be available to you by stepping out into an unknown direction or learning something new? What does it cost you to stay in the safe harbor of your existing path or career?

4. Who can help coach and guide you as you embrace an unknown future?

CHAPTER SEVEN

To Strive through Ambiguity

Why go purposely toward discomfort and terror? For what possible reason? The response is difficult at best, but I'm sure a person is an adventurer in direct proportion to the shortness of his or her memory. Somehow we sift out the bad times, remembering only the good ones of friendship, beauty, accomplishment, self-sufficiency, and the successful calculation of risk.

—Ned Gillette, adventurer, photographer, journalist, and author

In order to grow into the skills of an Expeditionary Leader you must be willing to face adversity. Outward Bound itself was born during a time of adversity and as an antidote to complacency. Adversity creates an openness to learning. It is why we leave the comfort of the known for the uncertainty and discomfort that come with any venture.

Outward Bound uses the wilderness as a source of adversity because most people have limited experience of being in such an environment. The unknown variables of the wilderness quickly heighten the disequilibrium that participants experience, testing their resolve and pushing them to discover new ways of being and leading.

In deciding to leave Outward Bound for a career in politics, former US congressman and senator Mark Udall demonstrated how adversity can create strong leaders. Mark compared the challenges of running for political office to his experiences as a seasoned mountaineer:

> Adventure has an unknown outcome. In order to have adventure you have to be willing to take some risks. I always found in life that I always learned a lot more from decisions that perhaps were wrong or ill advised than I have from the decisions that were right.
>
> I learned a lot more from mountains when I didn't finish the climb than I did from the mountains when I did reach the peak. It's the expeditions where you fall short, where you do some soul-searching, and look at the choices, and look to see what you might have done differently.

People can relate to overcoming the challenge of a peak ascent or running a rapid. More subtle yet often more impactful than the physical challenges are the personal and interpersonal challenges that people experience within themselves and with each other. These are often the place of lasting change on an individual level.

Mark continued:

> For me, physical risks have always been easier to take on than emotional risks or intellectual risks. Outward Bound shows that to a lot of people, because often the most challenging part about Outward Bound is being a part of the group. What's your place? How do you fit in? How do you deal with conflict?
>
> I really grew as an instructor and then as a leader in Outward Bound by being a part of those conflicts and learning—understanding how you embrace that tension for the purpose of learning and growing. How you bring it up in a way that doesn't make things even more intense, even more dysfunctional. The more real you are with who you are, the more willing you are to say, "Look I am far from perfect here, and I was maybe short with you last night, and I apologize, but also, here's what I'm getting from you. Let's see if we can't work this out."

Mark discovered another fundamental truth of Expeditionary Leadership during his time at the Colorado Outward Bound School, where he eventually became the executive director. If you hold true to the values of the expedition and focus on people's growth, even something as adverse as having to dismiss someone from a job can offer important lessons.

"People liked me as a leader, but they also knew that if a line was crossed, Udall wasn't slow to remove that person," Mark said of those he had let go.

> I had a few instructors who later got back to me and thanked me because they were struggling in their personal lives and it was being reflected in their work performance. In all the cases that I'm aware of, these people turned their lives around after leaving Outward Bound. That was something we were always on the lookout for—people who'd become complacent. Every organization faces those kinds of challenges.

What Lies at the End of Adversity

Delaney Reynolds is not your typical teenager. In addition to playing sports and spending time with friends, Delaney operates an international nonprofit, has addressed the United Nations General Assembly, and serves on an international youth leadership council. At age fifteen she had her first Outward Bound experience, and from it, she learned a deep lesson about personal resolve through adversity.

As a high school student in Miami, Florida, Delaney signed up for a program called the Academy of Agents of Change, a unique educational approach based on Outward Bound principles and social entrepreneurship codesigned by Expeditionary Leader Eduardo Balarezo. The program is supported by Patricia Woodson, whose long history with both Outward Bound and entrepreneurship makes her a remarkable champion of the educational program. (More on her later.)

Right before Delaney's planned trip to Ecuador and the Galápagos Islands with the Academy of Agents of Change, she tore her ACL knee ligament playing basketball.

"Initially the school told me that I couldn't go on the trip," Delaney recalled. "I was not going to have that. I had been planning for this trip for almost a year. I was so excited. I was going to physical therapy three times a week, sometimes more, to be able to build the muscle back in my leg just so I could go on this trip."

Ultimately, Delaney was cleared by her doctor to attend the trip to Ecuador and the Galápagos Islands and was able to participate fully with the other students. The grit she developed through the injury, her recovery, and her experience with Outward Bound was then directed at her passion to help save the environment.

> After I tore my ACL, I had a lot more free time. I initially got into a state of depression. I honestly didn't know what to do without basketball because I loved playing it so much. I decided to pour myself into the environmental project that I had started: The Sink or Swim Project. I took all this free time I had and I poured myself into climate change—interviewing even more people, and doing more presentations.
>
> Because of [the Academy of Agents of Change] I was able to learn about branding, I was able to learn about how to present my project in the correct way. That is one of the things I am most proud of. I was able to overcome such a significant obstacle and create what I have created today.

The Sink or Swim Project is a nonprofit connecting young people around the world to combat the negative effects of climate change and sea level rise. As the founder of the organization, Delaney has been called "one of the leading voices for the environment" by Philippe Cousteau, environmentalist and grandson of famed explorer Jacques Cousteau.

Patricia Woodson offers another great example of how Expeditionary Leaders pull from the inner resolve and grit necessary to strive through the unknown. Pat was one of the first female Outward Bound instructors. She then went on to become a photo journalist, when she butted up against the challenge of trying to share her work with other photographers. As a result, Pat cofounded Photo.net, the first photo-exchange service for professional photographers. Photo.net became the primary resource for *National Geographic* and grew to serve clients in twenty-three countries. Pat ran the business for a dozen years as CEO, selling it as the internet began to take off. She was one of the first successful women entrepreneurs in the rising tech space and credited her experience as a mountaineer and wilderness instructor for giving her the inner strength to succeed in the male-dominated business world.

As an Expeditionary Leader you learn that adversity accelerates learning, that it is often the catalyst for the greatest growth for both team and leader. That was certainly my experience while working for the Grappone Companies. We had recently begun a conversion to a new sales process, and as the director of corporate potential, I managed our training department. We were also working with a consulting company that provided training. During one of the training weeks the president and owner of the company called me in at the end of a workday. The trainer that was supposed to be working with us the next day was unable to make it. They told me that I had to take over the training myself. Though I had been supporting the training process, I had never led it. And I had never worked in auto sales. Now I was responsible for delivering the training course with less than twenty-four hours' notice.

That was the first of many training programs I delivered. A year and a half later, I was promoted to director of sales for the company. The adversity of that moment allowed me to step up to the plate. I was called to pull on my strengths and push myself into the unknown. Without that adversity, I doubt the opportunity to become sales director would have ever arisen, and I wouldn't have been able to serve in the way that I did.

REFLECTION

1. Which story or stories in the chapter most resonate with you and why?

2. What adversity have you faced in your life? What has it taught you?

3. What adversity are you currently facing in your life or work? How might that adversity help you to grow?

4. On a scale of 1 to 10, where would you rate yourself on your grit and determination? What can you do to strengthen your resilience?

5. Who is your "resilience coach"? How does she or he help you learn? If you don't currently have one, where might you find guidance?

CHAPTER EIGHT

To Strive for Your Values

Each time a man stands for an ideal, or acts to improve the lot of others, or strikes out against injustice, he sends forth a tiny ripple of hope. And crossing each other from a million different centers of energy and daring, those ripples build a current that can sweep down the mightiest walls of oppression and resistance.

—Robert F. Kennedy

For more than fifty years Outward Bound has developed leaders steeped in the values of integrity, mentorship, and compassion. While research on these important values has been around for decades, they are only now beginning to be fully integrated into organizational practices, particularly in business. Books such as *Good to Great* have identified the importance of humble, compassionate leaders. Yet most of our organizations still struggle with this view of leadership. As an October 2018 *Harvard Business Review* article headline so succinctly asked, "If Humility Is So Important, Why Are Leaders So Arrogant?"

Integrity: Showing Up as You Are

When you are with someone twenty-four hours a day for the duration of a wilderness expedition, it's impossible to be anything but who you really are. Being humble and human are leadership values that Michael Welp, the founder of White Men as Full Diversity Partners, learned from his time at Outward Bound. Mark Udall also credits Outward Bound for the type of authentic leadership he modeled as a politician:

> In the Congress I looked to bring a lot of role modeling that was based on Outward Bound principles. You have power by how you carry yourself and what you do. It's not what you say. It's what you do.
>
> You don't schmooze your way up a mountain, you climb the damn thing. You don't trash-talk your way up a mountain. You lead openly, you lead in all of these respects, you praise publicly, you punish privately, you value everybody. I tried to carry myself and project a persona that reflected Outward Bound values.

Mentoring: Sharing the Learnings

Outward Bound leaders work almost exclusively in pairs. Can an expedition be successful with a solo leader? Yes, but something of significance is then lost—a big part of the leader's learning.

During the planning phase of an Outward Bound experience, two leaders come together to plan the physical route of the trip, organize the logistics (gear, food, drop-offs and pick-ups, etc.), and review the files of the participants. They also spend a great deal of time getting to know each other, discussing their strengths and weaknesses, and setting their own goals for the expedition. Often there are lead and assistant roles, but even in full partnerships each leader focuses on fostering the other's growth. The mentoring that goes along with this relationship is part of the power and magic of an Outward Bound experience for the leaders as well as the participants.

> Never be an opportunist. Be an opportunity seeker for others.

Those words from William "Bill" Sloane Coffin Jr., who ran training for the first Peace Corps volunteers, are burned into the memory of his mentee Richard Holzman. Richard has the distinction of having participated in the first Outward Bound experience in the United States as part of the inaugural class of then President John F. Kennedy's newly formed Peace Corps.

Richard and Bill maintained a relationship for the rest of Bill's life. Bill became a major leader in the civil rights and peace movements of the sixties and seventies. Richard began a lifetime career as an educator and administrator, leading school districts in New Jersey, New York, and Massachusetts. He became the director of the American International School in Caracas, Venezuela, and later a university dean in Massachusetts. In each place Richard landed, Bill would visit his faculty and students. His passion for mentoring lasted throughout his life.

"Bill always said, 'The way you show gratitude is you let other people climb on your shoulders.' That's what he taught me. And I've tried to pass that on in everything I've done in my life. That's why I continued to be involved with Outward Bound throughout the years." Richard recounted.

One person that Richard mentored was Scott Hartl. When they met, Scott was working as a river raft guide in Utah, and Richard was serving as superintendent of the Schenectady, New York, school system. Together, they developed a collaborative experiential education program with Cooperstown, a fairly rural town not far from Schenectady. In Cooperstown, Richard said, there was

> a lot of beauty and wealth, but a lot of poverty as well. And in Schenectady, we had everything from research scientists' children to poor African Americans and other kids—a real diverse community—and we wanted to show them the world beyond their immediate environments. We had kids canoeing on the Mohawk

River to see their city from a different perspective, from the water. Conversely, we took these kids from Cooperstown and brought them to Schenectady.

Scott went on to become a founding member and the president and CEO of EL Education, an offshoot of Outward Bound that brings expeditionary learning principles to school systems. It is currently used by fifty thousand students in one hundred thirty schools across thirty states. Much like Outward Bound founder Kurt Hahn, Richard has been a bit of a "midwife" of ideas, contributing to the development of programs and then letting them take their own course.

"Whatever you are doing has to have meaning and be about serving others," said Richard. "It's not just about oneself. It's about self and relationship to others. That's the legacy I'm hoping I leave to the world. It's not platitudes. It's the way you live your life."

Compassion: Alleviating the Suffering of Others

The capstone of a successful Expeditionary Leader's journey is deep respect, connection, and caring for self, for others, and for the environment in which we live. The expedition cannot achieve success if individuals do not have compassion for each other.

Compassion comes in two parts. The first is a deep understanding of and sympathy for the challenges and suffering of others. You could call that empathy. That connection is critical for an Expeditionary Leader, but it is only the first step. The second requires action. Expeditionary Leaders take action to alleviate that suffering. Empathy and action together form the true measure of distinction of an Expeditionary Leader. Outward Bound teaches this to its participants and demands it of its leaders—both during an expedition and in their daily lives.

"The fact that it's experiential is very powerful," said Laura Kohler, senior vice president of stewardship and sustainability for Kohler Co.

> It's not just reading a book on compassion. It's practicing compassion in the hardest moments, when you don't even like the person you have to be compassionate for. And whether you're talking about an urban immersion in NYC with youth, a three-week course, a semester course, or a professional group, it's all transferable to your professional life or your personal life.

Expeditionary Leaders understand the responsibility they carry to live in a place of compassion. That is because among the Outward Bound pillars, compassion stands above all. It's also a by-product of developing Outward Bound's other core values. Without integrity, a willingness to share and learn together, and respect for each person's journey, compassion is very difficult to foster.

As a certified personal coactive coach and an Outward Bound leader with more than a thousand days in the field, I have lived in the space of deep compassion and connection. I worked to model and teach compassion as I led the sales and training functions of an auto dealer group and saw a completely unique organization build itself on integrity, kindness, and respect.

For example, new hires at Grappone attend a culture training. This is their introduction to the unique company they have joined, one that emphasizes care of the team member. Profits are a by-product of treating everyone with integrity, kindness, and respect. Many new employees are stunned at the intentionality that is behind the company's actions. If they have worked at other auto dealer groups, they are often in disbelief. If this can be done in the cut-throat world of auto sales, it can be done anywhere. In an industry where the average turnover among sales departments is above 70 percent, Grappone has had years when the turnover on its sales floors was below 15 percent.

REFLECTION

1. Which story or stories in the chapter most resonate with you and why?

2. What are your values? What's really important to you on a deep level? How present are these values in your day-to-day work and life? Where are they missing or not being served? How can you pull them more deeply into what you do?

3. What can do right now to offer more empathy and compassion to others?

4. Who can help support you in this?

Not to Yield

I have an expression, "There is no finish line."
That connects with the Outward Bound notion
of "not to yield."
    —Arthur Blank

Not to yield: This is resilience. Outward Bound teaches people that they are capable of so much more than they may realize—as long as they never give up. Expeditionary Leadership is about developing character. Armed with that knowledge and a sense of responsibility for their fellow travelers and the planet, they know when to take a stand. As the hardest minerals and toughest steel are forged under heat and pressure, so too are the qualities of the Expeditionary Leaders.

In addition, not yielding speaks to not accepting the status quo. Expeditionary Leaders are always striving toward a greater ideal. They follow a compass point, not an end point.

CHAPTER NINE

Not Yielding to Uncertainty

Always in the big woods, when you leave familiar ground and step off alone into a new place there will be, along with feelings of curiosity and excitement, a little nagging dread. It is the ancient fear of the Unknown, and it is your first bond with the wilderness you are going into. What you are doing is exploring. You are undertaking the first experience, not of the place, but of yourself in that place. It is an experience of essential loneliness; for nobody can discover the world for anybody else. It is only after we have discovered it for ourselves that it becomes a common ground and bond, and we cease to be alone.

 —Wendell Berry

Expeditionary Leaders are, at their heart, adventurers. Underpinning that adventure is deep trust and confidence in the people they are leading. In the years I spent leading wilderness trips for Outward Bound, whether setting out on a corporate leadership program or a semester-long program for college students, we all experienced that same moment of fear and uncertainty, and then, collectively, we made the decision to move forward anyway.

As Laura Kohler of Kohler Co. put it: "When there is no way out, you have to say, 'OK, one foot in front of the other. This is the only way I'm going to get out of this really uncomfortable situation.' It's just cutting down the noise, focusing on the issue, and really putting one foot in front of the other."

I can recall an Outward Bound trip where we were in the midst of a particularly difficult stretch of trail in the Chisos Mountains in Big Bend National Park, West Texas. We had traveled eastward for a few days in the desert following a pretty steady contour to the south of the mountains. We reached the eastern side, and the trail hooked north and then west. What followed was a 3,200-foot elevation gain in only a few miles. There was no shade and no water until we reached the top.

At the midpoint of the hike a participant doubled over, hands on his knees and sucking air into his chest. He looked at me in deep distress and asked, "Isn't this hard for you?"

I smiled. "Of course, it's hard for me," I responded, noticing the soreness where my backpack rested on my hips and the familiar feeling of aching calves and tired feet. "The only difference between us is that I have been here before."

Experience had taught me that it is not the physical challenge that makes an Outward Bound trip so daunting; it is the experience that goes on inside our minds as we face the unknown. Moreover, it is the will to keep on going regardless that determines our success. My job was to guide the team and myself on our journey without yielding to the uncertainty we would inevitably face.

Expeditionary Leaders hold a tremendous responsibility to themselves, their organizations, and their communities. As the author and conservationist Liz Cunningham so aptly put it,

> Leadership ultimately is about doing what is right and inspiring other people to do what is right as well. Leaders might not always be the best communicators. They might not always be that easy to get along with. They may be a little bit cryptic. They may doubt themselves terribly. But in a very critical moment they do the right thing and inspire other people to do it.

I see Expeditionary Leadership as a calling to a lifelong journey of human development. Unlike most forms of traditional education and leadership, Expeditionary Leaders are trained to be grounded, to watch for teachable moments, and to adapt to the situation. They light the path in the darkness, and they also walk it with grit and dedication.

• • •

A fifteen-passenger van full of leaders and participants journeys down a bumpy dirt road, stopping at a trailhead. The group forms a circle around the leaders, suitcases at their feet. Clothing and provisions are checked to make sure everyone is equipped for the journey. Gear is distributed and packed into backpacks with clothing. The suitcases are closed and returned to the van. The group stands together and watches as the van pulls away, the rattling and engine noises fading to the powerful silence of the wilderness. This is the moment when the leaders and participants have become "outward bound."

For a leader this is a watershed moment. Outward Bound participants are not experienced wilderness travelers. Most have never even camped, let alone been in deep wilderness. The unknown creates a deep sense of disequilibrium with the participants, an off-balance feeling that is often the precursor to transformation.

By design, Outward Bound experiences are transformative—their impact goes far beyond the initial experience to change the way the participants deal with uncertainty in their everyday lives. Michael Welp of White Men as Full Diversity Partners has applied his Outward Bound experiences to the design of his diversity seminars to ensure they yield similar results.

"We've been able to touch many different parts of the organization and create that change where white men are owning their privilege, and educating each other, and challenging each other, and intervening on gender dynamics before women are even aware that they have changed," Michael said.

> After twenty years of doing this work, I know it's going to be transformative, and I don't have to do all the challenging myself because the situation and design does it. The same thing happens at an Outward Bound course. It's not the Outward Bound instructors who have to do that; they're just midwifing the learning through the rock climbing and the bugs and components of the course.

Expeditionary Leaders immerse themselves in these deeply transformative experiences. As a wilderness instructor and a corporate coach, I have experienced it again and again. Even for the leaders—whether it's an expedition, a new "stretch assignment," or a change initiative—the trip is rife with uncertainty and opportunities to grow. Knowing that helps you to keep going until you reach your goal.

Finding More in Yourself than You Know

For the individual, the journey of not yielding is about discovering the inner strength and resolve to perform at a much higher level. In a wilderness context that realization comes at the pinnacle of a personal challenge. Expeditionary Leaders guide that individual growth without judgment.

"You metaphorically push people out of their comfort zones," said Peter Bailey of the strategic planning and leadership development firm Prouty Project.

Laura Kohler of Kohler Co. faced such a challenge when she joined her family's business and also joined the national board of Outward Bound years after leaving her Outward Bound instructor career. Laura's father had been on the board of Outward Bound in the United States. When he retired from the board, he told them he wanted Laura to take his seat.

"I think they reluctantly put me on the board. I was a good ten to fifteen years younger than everybody else. So I came on the board, and for the first year they didn't even talk to me," she recounted. Even within an organization as successful as Outward Bound there are opportunities to move through discomfort and uncertainty and discover more about what you are capable of.

> Finally, there was a meeting in Chicago and I walked up to two of the people running the show on the board. I said, "Look,

I have a lot of skills. I'm head of HR at a big company, I have three hundred people around the world that I deploy. We have thirty-five thousand people. I can do something. And I'm the only person on the board who was an instructor. If you don't use me, I'm stepping off the board because this is a waste of my time."

Speaking up for herself brought Laura into the fold and she was eventually nominated to be the vice chair and then the chair of Outward Bound USA. Laura's time as board chair has been transformational for the organization, and it is a living example of using one's learning as an Outward Bound participant and instructor to not yield to personal challenges.

My first opportunity to blend Outward Bound with organizational leadership came with Cox Enterprises, an Atlanta-based conglomerate that owns media companies, communications companies, and automotive services such as Autotrader and Manheim Auctions. Cox executives ran independent business units, such as television stations or an auto auction. Each executive had to demonstrate a combination of independence and interdependence in order to succeed as a leader at Cox.

Gordon French, who was Cox's director of executive development, used Outward Bound to begin the Expeditionary Leadership process for the company's executives. He recognized that the wilderness experience would open them to new ways of thinking and responding, that the uncertainty of the wilderness terrain mirrored the uncertainty of leading a business unit. The purpose of the program was to enable Cox leaders to operate successfully in a unique, decentralized, entrepreneurial organization during periods of rapid change.

Through 360-degree feedback and business measurements, Gordon garnered millions of dollars in positive impact on Cox business units by bringing their leaders through the Outward Bound program. The adversity experienced in the wilderness expeditions was used as a metaphor for the work environment, and daily de-briefings were designed to focus on transferring the experience to the day-to-day challenges each executive faced.

Staying in the comfort of the known is easy. Most people perceive that there is risk in the unknown. But Expeditionary Leaders understand that in this ever-changing world, staying put actually poses a greater risk. Uncertainty is the guide that leads us to our greatest strengths.

REFLECTION

1. Which story or stories in the chapter most resonate with you and why?

2. How have you responded when faced with uncertainty in past situations? What have you learned about yourself?

3. Is there an uncertain situation in your life right now? What might be available to you by stepping into the uncertainty?

4. What story or stories do you notice in your head when things become uncertain? What things can you do to change that story?

5. Who in your life can help you to lead through uncertainty?

CHAPTER TEN

Not Yielding to What's Easy

The ultimate measure of a man is not where he stands in moments of comfort and convenience, but where he stands at times of challenge and controversy.
—Martin Luther King Jr.

A n Expeditionary Leader's sense of responsibility is anchored in the courage to stand up for something larger than oneself. Outward Bound founder Kurt Hahn modeled this courage in his own life when he openly challenged Hitler and the nationalism that was spreading across his home country of Germany. He didn't take the easy way out; he stood up for what he believed in at his own peril. In fact, he was thrown in jail for it. Supporters of Hahn were eventually able to get him released and out of Nazi Germany. He then worked to get his sister and her family—who were half Jewish—out of the country as well.

This deep sense of responsibility to others and society, this ability to show up even during difficult times, is a signature characteristic of an Expeditionary Leader.

Our youngest Expeditionary Leader, Delaney Reynolds, has made it her mission to show up for her beliefs in the face of opposition. As the founder of The Sink or Swim Project, a nongovernmental environmental organization, she connects young people around the world to shine the light on the negative effects of climate change. Delaney said:

> Standing in Miami, my home city, in rain boots and sloshing through saltwater is really difficult because I know it's only going to get worse in the future. As seas continue to get higher, water is going to continue to move more and more inland.
>
> There's a statistic that Miami-Dade County floods about six times per year up to midlevel calves—really bad sea-level rise. I've seen that change in my short lifetime. That hasn't happened historically. By 2030 it's going to flood 80 times per year. By 2045 it's going to flood 380 times per year—sometimes more than once per day. That threatens my home in the Keys, my home in Miami, my institution where I go to school, and families all over South Florida, especially those who can't move.
>
> It's really frustrating to watch this happening and see people who are in power—who could do so much to help us—ignore it. And it's not just a Florida issue, even though we are ground zero for sea-level rise. This is a global issue. No matter where you are, you're going to be affected some way.

Delaney has vowed to focus on addressing the problem of rising sea levels. Starting her own nonprofit was not easy, but now her Sink or Swim Project is modeling for others how even teenagers can make an impact in their community if they are passionate about something.

What is so extraordinary about Delaney is twofold: first, that she cares so deeply about her greater community and, second, that she takes action when the moment calls for it, as she did when she called out Miami officials for not taking the climate change problem seriously.

At fifteen, Delaney decided that she needed to speak at the Miami-Dade County commission meeting. Delaney's father was driving her there, and it started pouring. There were manhole covers lifting off the streets. She recalled:

I'm just typing away in the passenger seat writing my thoughts. I hadn't planned ahead of the time to go; it was kind of a whim thing. I was like, "Let's go," and my dad was like, "OK."

We're driving there, and I am furiously typing away, and when we get there there's probably two hundred people in the chambers. I was very nervous. But I got up and I spoke in front of the entire commission and the mayor. I asked them to allocate a million dollars [to the problem of sea rise]. When I did that they actually all started laughing at me. Like that was a ridiculous amount. I explained that even a million dollars isn't enough to solve the problem, but we need to start somewhere.

Later that day, the commission allocated $300,000 and created a new position called the chief resiliency officer for the county. Later they increased the budget to $1.2 million, and now the budget for countering sea level rise is $1.7 million. The chief resiliency officer has also asked Delaney to sit on a steering committee that is specifically focused on environmental issues in Miami-Dade County.

"I don't think I would have been able to get up in front of the commission and the mayor had it not been for the lessons Outward Bound taught me in working with other people and speaking in front of people. I'm really grateful for that," Delany said. In addition, Outward Bound taught Delaney the importance of standing up for something that mattered to her. Her care for the people of Miami-Dade County and her commitment to protecting the environment are the product of her early immersion in Outward Bound's character-development initiatives.

Grit

In the world of business, grit is an elusive value: highly sought after yet easily compromised by the desire we humans have for a sense of belonging. For so many, the need to belong overrides our convictions, and we end up disregarding our values to be a part of the group. More than anything else, this leads to the erosion of our freedoms and creates the self-imposed limitations that lead to the greatest waste in the world—the waste of human potential. At best, this waste leads to uninspired workplaces and disengaged employees doing unfulfilling work. At worst, it allows for the rise of totalitarian leaders and the horrors that Hahn foresaw in Germany as Hitler rose to power.

To be an Expeditionary Leader means to stand in a place of personal values, just as former US congressman and senator Mark Udall did. Mark was motivated to run for office because he felt compelled to stand up for what he thought was right. He stood in his place of truth, fighting to uphold America's ideals—like not torturing people—even though that stance was not popular shortly after the September 11, 2001, terrorist attacks.

> I stood up to the Central Intelligence Agency and the use of enhanced interrogations, which I saw as torture. I believe how we conduct ourselves sends a message and is reflective of what our core values are. I felt there was a contradiction between what our core values are and what our actions were.
>
> I could have kept my head down, but I ultimately voted against giving the CIA director that authority to use enhanced interrogation techniques. I believed it was the wrong strategy. I was very outspoken and amongst the minority: those who voted no.

By voting no, Mark ran the risk of being seen as weak, as not standing up for the thousands who were murdered in the September 11 attacks. But he had the grit to refuse the easier path that went against his convictions. In addition, he voted against giving President George W. Bush the authority to go to war in Iran, another unpopular position at the time. Mark considered these to be some of the most consequential things he has ever done that reflect the theme of not yielding. When you believe something is not right, you stand your ground and accept the consequences. Outward Bound founder Kurt Hahn believed that this fundamental lesson would create an enlightened citizenry that is always prepared to do the right thing.

Mark explained:

> You're going to be seen as not understanding the world, you're going to be seen as naive, you're not going to have the chance to be elected statewide, which I was beginning to consider. And a lot of people were urging me to run for the United States Senate. But all of those concerns took a back seat to what I considered the right course of action.
>
> It was a risk, less quantifiable than falling off a mountain or drowning in a river, but no less significant a risk to my career. I'm proud that I cast that vote and didn't slink away.

Delaney and Mark are both shining examples of what Outward Bound and Expeditionary Leadership produce. Perhaps the best description of this is a saying that was written by Bob Pieh, who founded the Minnesota Outward Bound School (now Voyageur Outward Bound) and later brought Outdoor Experiential Education to Canada.

The saying is carved on wooden signs posted on trees as you turn onto the mile-long dirt road to Homeplace, the Voyageur Outward Bound School base.

> Be Tough, Yet Gentle. Humble, Yet Bold.
> Swayed Always by Beauty and Truth.

REFLECTION

1. Which story or stories in the chapter most resonate with you and why?

2. What does "not yielding" mean to you?

3. What areas of potential discomfort are you avoiding in your life? What do you have to gain by staying comfortable? What might you gain by stepping into discomfort?

4. What cause most calls you? How could you make a difference by leaning into it and not yielding to the temptation of the status quo? When will you act?

5. Where in your life are you taking the easy path right now? What will you do to challenge yourself?

CHAPTER ELEVEN

Not Yielding to Doubt

Our deepest fear is not that we are inadequate. Our deepest fear is that we are powerful beyond belief. It is our light, not our darkness, that most frightens us. We ask ourselves, "Who am I to be brilliant, gorgeous, talented, and fabulous?" Actually, who are you not to be?

—Marianne Williamson

As a participant on an Outward Bound course, Rue Mapp, the founder of Outdoor Afro, experienced a teachable moment that left an indelible mark on her life. "Even though I had a lot of nature experience, I didn't have any mountaineering experience," Rue said. "I felt I was in pretty good shape because I was riding my bike all of the time. I had a pretty active lifestyle. I thought I was going to be all right in that regard."

Outward Bound sends participants a list of clothing and equipment to bring on a wilderness trip. Rue decided she didn't need one particular item that was recommended.

"I didn't bring my headlamp because where I came from, we used flashlights," recalled Rue. "So why do I need a headlamp?"

Rue learned why she needed a headlamp fairly early on her Outward Bound trip, which was a mountaineering course in California. On one of the first evenings after a practice climb, the group was going to stay overnight on the rock. Rue had to go up first because she didn't have a head lamp.

"I was really slow and scared. As I felt my way up, I was losing light on the other side of the mountain. About halfway up I couldn't really see anymore. I remember being terrified and feeling like I couldn't go through with it. I was crying and I was definitely at my end with it," she recounted.

Just when she felt like giving up, her instructor leaned over and said, "Rue, just trust your feet."

"That was a very powerful moment that awakened something inside of me, that helped me to scramble to the top. I took that much later as a powerful lesson of having faith in yourself that you could dig in and you could go forward with what you have. What you have is enough."

Trusting your feet and not yielding to self-doubt. Rue has returned to that mantra again and again in her life and career. It became part of her leadership DNA as she began developing African American leaders across the United States.

> That was exactly the lesson that I needed to learn at the precipice of adulthood. I'm still trusting my feet. I am still having moments when I don't know what just happened, and I don't know what is going to happen, but I can still dig in and have that kind of faith.
>
> "Trust your feet" has been a living mantra for me. I don't always know where the path will lead me. I don't feel like I always have all the tools. Or the resources. Or the skills. But all of those things are available through belief and faith. That's what happened. That's what got me up that mountain.

That teachable moment has continued to get Rue up the mountains in her life ever since.

I believe it's important to highlight the leadership gem that lies at the heart of Rue's story. Rue made a decision to not bring a headlamp. Her Outward Bound instructors could have bailed her out by supplying her with one. Instead her leaders chose to let her experience the consequences of her choice. If they had not done that, she wouldn't have been first up on that climb, nor would she have faced that moment of extreme fear when darkness fell. She would not have learned to "trust her feet," perhaps missing out on one of the most significant lessons of her life. Rue's Outward Bound leader believed in her, particularly when she was at that moment of doubt and did not believe in herself. Leading this way requires a deep reverence for the process. Expeditionary Leaders know the value of trusting their people and allowing them to experience the consequences of their choices—to exercise their life muscles, as Rue put it.

Building That Life Muscle

"Outward Bound gave me the start of building that muscle that through life experience has become stronger and made me more willing to take risks," Rue said.

> There was a part of me that was like, "I could play it safe and stay in my great program officer job at the foundation, or I could take a risk in starting my own company. . . ."
>
> I had a friend who was very thoughtful, and she said, "I think you're ready. It's time you step off. And if you step off, the net will appear." It was really terrifying with three little kids to do something like start a new business, to say I'm going to make a whole career out of something I'm really passionate about, in the absence of any savings, or really anything. It's a lot of different things in play. Just recently it feels like the parachute has opened.

Rue's journey is an example of the Outward Bound lessons applied: Get clear about what you stand for and never yield to doubt. The success of Outdoor Afro is a testament to her early lessons of trusting her feet, discovering her purpose, and following it into the unknown.

Laura Kohler of Kohler Co. agreed that her Outward Bound experiences strengthened her ability to stand up to doubt—in nature and in her corporate job—and to forge forward anyway.

There were days on my Outward Bound course when I was sixteen that were really challenging, whether it was because it was the weather, or the lack of food, or because I was one of only two teenagers on the course and everybody else was adult, mostly male.

There were times when I thought I couldn't go on. And today there are times when it's so hard and I just have to slow down and stop and say, "I can do this. I did it then. I made it to the end then. I can do more than I realize."

For Maggie Fox, past president of The Climate Reality Project, The Climate Action Fund, and America Votes, building her life muscles is a never-ending mission. Her entire career reflects her wonderment of being engaged on an Expeditionary Leadership journey.

I'm a student over and over again. I keep moving through life and changing, and I have to meet myself again; I have to figure out this new part of me that's emerging. There's a fundamental humility to it but also a confidence.

The deeper you know yourself, the better you become at what you do. You become more confident, you become stronger. First you learn that you can be a leader. Then, what kind of leader am I? Who am I in this? The whole notion of leader as learner is at the heart of this. The humility and curiosity that comes from leading and learning at the same time is the key. At the core I am always a learner.

Michael Welp of White Men as Full Diversity Partners echoed Maggie's sentiment: "I will always have this sense of humbleness that I have plenty to learn. I'm always looking for the learning edge in myself."

One of Maggie's greatest joys as a leader has come from helping others learn to trust their feet and build their own life muscles. "Being an instructor was the biggest gift of my life," she said. "How magical is it to watch people kind of fall in love with themselves, to learn 'I'm a good person. I can do this.' That sense of wonder about yourself that is so rare. Having the experience of watching people unfold into their own beauty and power. They rise. Like a fish to a lure, they rise."

Being an Expeditionary Leader, Maggie said, is about knowing how to extend that invitation to others to unfold, to rise. "You're going to get magic every time. You just do. And it's not because you're magical; it's because you gave them the chance to be something they want to be."

Maggie's husband, former senator Mark Udall, also reflected on the deep importance of developing people and relationships, especially in times of adversity like his loss in the 2014 Colorado Senate election. "It was heartbreaking to lose the Colorado Senate seat, but one of the things that gave me the greatest satisfaction was that I had built this team of just amazing people whose responsibility was to the entire state of Colorado," he said.

Mark modeled his commitment to his people after his defeat by spending the next six months helping his staff find new jobs in a number of vocations.

> If the people who worked for me had a different opportunity to work for someone else or do something that gave them a chance to grow and have more responsibility, it was important for me to always support that. That's Outward Bound. You're always looking to give your students more and more responsibility. Your job is to make yourself obsolete.
>
> Your job is to have them be "outward bound" fully, where if they don't have the skills, they have the confidence in getting the skills, and they have the skills tied to understanding yourself and how to work with people, how to find that motivation.

It is through this focus on and belief in people that Expeditionary Leaders are able to not yield to doubt. Trusting the process is just the same as trusting your feet. It is knowing that you as well as the people you lead are far more capable than any of you realize.

REFLECTION

1. Which story or stories in this chapter most resonate with you and why?

2. What doubts have come up for you as you've stepped into something new or big or considered making a bigger impact on the world?

3. Where in life can you "trust your feet"?

4. Who can you call on to support you in building your life muscles?

5. Who can you support as they learn to trust their own feet and build their life muscles?

What Do These Keys Unlock?

Outward Bound has come to mean many things in different places and for the great variety of people who are drawn to it. But at its heart, in every time and place, is Hahn's own center, his conviction that it is possible, even in a relatively short time, to introduce greater balance and compassion into human lives by impelling people into experiences which show them they can rise above adversity and overcome their own defeatism. They can make more of their lives than they thought they could, and learn to serve others with their strength.

—Thomas James, Provost and Dean of the Teachers College,
Columbia University

When an Outward Bound course is complete, the group gathers together for the final time. Typically in a circle, they stand and share their learning and appreciation for each other. More likely than not, they are left with an important message: Even though this particular trip is complete, the journey is really just beginning. They have discovered the keys to something bigger— and it is up to them what they unlock. As Arthur Blank so aptly stated, "There is no finish line."

A common thread among all of the Expeditionary Leaders who contributed to this book is that they use those keys to unlock their purpose in this world, to find their unique way of contributing to a more vibrant global community. Living like this brings "connectedness to life and purpose and meaning," said Richard Holzman, senior adviser for the University of Massachusetts, Amherst's College of Education, and one of Outward Bound's first participants. It is the opposite of the alienation that so many in our society are experiencing today and that has led to so much divisiveness and disconnection.

Richard explained:

> At first it was Outward Bound in the natural environment. Then it grew into, "Gee, if we can do that, we can create the same environment in an urban experience. This is how you can help move society forward. This is how we can integrate people who have differences, right in their home communities, if you create the right experiences."
>
> People meet—in many instances they begin as total strangers—and share an experience, full of adversity and challenge, and they will always remember these experiences. I want to pass it on because it has had a deep connection to me, to my emotions, my spirit, and my growth as a substantive human being.

Richard spent most of his career in education because passing on his knowledge is his way of being of service.

> One of the lessons I learned is that the way you show gratitude is you let other people climb on your shoulders. You are free with not only your money but with whatever you can contribute. Quite frankly, not enough people are generous with what they can do for others. I've interviewed a lot of teachers and administrators, and I'd often ask, "If this was the eleventh hour of your life, what would you want to be remembered for?" That was my way of assessing how committed they were to serving others. That has been what has sustained me throughout my whole career, the whole notion of servant leadership.

However, Richard also made it clear that education is not the only way to make a contribution. "There are opportunities for service whether you are in business or in the public sector. It just has to be something that's in your soul."

Laura Kohler of Kohler Co. agreed that a soulful commitment to service and a sense of purpose are the ties that bind all who have experienced Outward Bound.

> We come from different backgrounds, but fundamentally Outward Bound is a philosophy, a way of being, a way of leading. It is a culture, and if you have had an Outward Bound experience, you understand there's this coming together. I've seen it with boards that we meet around the US, I've seen it with instructors, I've seen it with students.
>
> That's why companies are starting to morph to purpose. People who are coming to companies and staying want a sense of purpose. Outward Bound is purposeful. It's building leaders for the future. It's building character in people.

People First

Outward Bound's greatest ideal is service to others. Arthur Blank, a Home Depot cofounder and the current owner of the Atlanta Falcons, cites service as an integral piece of the culture of every organization he has led.

By any definition Arthur's life has been a tremendous success. When he retired from The Home Depot as cochairman in 2001, he and partner Bernie Marcus had revolutionized the home improvement industry, launched the warehouse superstore revolution, and become billionaires.[1] As an independent trainer and coach, I had the chance to work with many of The Home Depot store and district managers through my affiliation with the North Carolina Outward Bound School. It amazed me how in a company as large as The

---

1. What is often overlooked in their success story is that Arthur and Bernie founded the Home Depot after they were fired from their previous jobs. In classic Expeditionary Leader fashion, they used adversity to fuel their next achievements.

Home Depot, there was such deep respect for Arthur. Many of the managers had stories of working as an associate early in their careers and encountering him walking the store aisles, straightening shelves. His enthusiasm for serving customers was legendary, and his presence made a significant impact on his associates.

"The greatest success at The Home Depot was not the store expansion," reflected Arthur.

> It was really the people. People who have been injected and infested and swallowed up by this orange-blooded philosophy of being of service to others. That is something you can't copy. It comes out of this notion of being in service to others. Being in service doesn't just mean on the outside; it means on the inside too. Not just serving the public but serving each other.
>
> That philosophy hasn't changed at all. Those core values that we built at The Home Depot are exactly the same ones that we use with all of my current companies. We're running all of these disconnected businesses, and our results have been extraordinarily good. They apply to a football team, a soccer team, the largest golf retail in the country, a couple of guest ranches out west, and to our foundation.
>
> All great businesses take responsibility for having a positive impact on their communities. You want associates to feel that this organization is worthy of their lives. It's not just a job. I don't go to work every day; I go to mission every day. I'm working, I'm playing, I'm connecting with people, I'm giving back. I work very, very hard at that.
>
> I think that the associates feel like the notion of giving back is very important. For associates it's critical that they feel like their organization is one that is engaged in making a difference in the world. It's human nature to want to serve and to be generous with their service. We're tapping into the essence of the way people are really wired to be.

Arthur touched on a critical linchpin of Expeditionary Leadership. Leaders see the greater purpose of work, and they bridge that purpose with the day-to-day actions of their team members. They create both the light and the path for others to follow.

Arthur followed his run at Home Depot by purchasing the struggling Atlanta Falcons for $545 million and turning it into a perennial favorite with an estimated value of $2.6 billion in 2018, according to *Forbes* magazine. In 2016 Arthur's company, AMB Group, assumed management of the newly opened Mercedes-Benz stadium, one of the most advanced sports venues in the world. With a retractable pinwheel roof and one of the largest LED screens in the world, it represents the pinnacle of success.

In the shadows of the stadium, however, are some of the most blighted, poor, crime-ridden areas in the city. This is where Arthur found his purpose anew.

> We didn't want the stadium to be in the shadow of those kinds of communities. We wanted the stadium to be in the shadows of communities that have been elevated. These neighborhoods are the birthplace of Martin Luther King Jr. They are the birthplace of the civil rights movement. It just wasn't OK.

The Arthur M. Blank Family Foundation is contributing $15 million for development in the historic neighborhoods surrounding the stadium. In addition, the foundation, in partnership with the North Carolina Outward Bound School and local Atlanta schools, has launched American Explorers, a yearlong leadership development program. The program offers youth from Atlanta's historic westside a highly intensive opportunity to learn the skills to become change agents, entrepreneurs, civic leaders, educators, and community stewards. It is here that Arthur puts most of his time and energy. On the American Explorers' website homepage is one of Arthur's favorite sayings: "There is no finish line."

Finding Your Path

Peter Bailey of the Prouty Project sees his entire life as an extended Outward Bound course. Through that lens, he is continually applying the lessons from his wilderness experiences to unlock more:

> To be on our own Outward Bound course. . . . If we're self-aware, we get to do that work. How am I being resilient? How am I confronting my own limiting beliefs? How am I recognizing my fears that are maybe unfounded? How am I bringing out my best self? Life continually throws stuff at us, with our kids, with our aging parents, with our partners.
>
> You hear people talking, "Ah, I got a flat tire on the way to work and god, my life sucks." Or, you could say, "Hey, kids, ever changed a flat tire before?" and see it as a learning opportunity. That's the Kurt Hahn thing: How do we see this as an opportunity to learn and serve in a new way? That's the mindset I've been able to journey through life with, and it's been a wonderful journey because of that.

On a personal note, Peter's wife was diagnosed with cancer a few years ago. His Outward Bound keys unlocked his ability to see this setback as an opportunity to serve, strive, and not to yield, for his family.

Peter's response to the news was, "OK, that's our call to adventure. Here's our road of challenges. Here are the guardians at the gate. Here's the achievement we had in that journey. And how do we come back and tell people about that?"

After thirty years of applying the life lessons of Outward Bound leadership, Peter feels as though he has found his flow. He is in the zone and fulfilling his purpose. That is what Outward Bound has unlocked for him:

> I don't have all the answers by any stretch, but I feel like I have learned how to build relationships with senior executives and

become more of an adviser than a trainer. I get to work with some pretty cool people in helping them think through solutions for their own companies. That helps me to see, you know what, I'm making a difference here. It's not about corporate X or corporate Y, I'm working with people to be better people, to be better at what they do.

Peter's advice to other leaders?

Lead where you are! Hold a deep belief in people that they are inherently good. Be a vulnerable leader and invite more of these dialogues for mutual understanding—not necessarily mutual agreement, but mutual understanding. There's a quote by Rumi: "Outside of right doing and wrong doing there is a field. I'll meet you there." That's my journey.

What Do These Keys Unlock for the Future of Outward Bound?

Liz Cunningham has a unique perspective on the potential impact of Outward Bound. As a descendant of its founder, Kurt Hahn, she has also practiced the lessons of her great-uncle as a conservationist. She noted:

> We're headed in this century into a period of unprecedented change: unprecedented destruction and the potential for unprecedented, positive transformation. For people who are involved with Outward Bound, it's important to play a leading role. It's important to remind ourselves that Outward Bound was born during World War II, at another time when the world was deemed to be going to hell. It's important to revisit those roots through that lens.

Since the founding of the first Outward Bound School in the US in 1962, the organization has evolved to meet the changing needs of young people and adults. Serving, striving, and never yielding has led Outward Bound in the US to a period of renewal and growth.

Today in the United States, Outward Bound is a national network of regional schools, united by a shared mission to "change lives through challenge and discovery." The network is governed by Outward Bound USA, ensuring consistency in safety, program quality, and the professional development of instructors. Outward Bound USA exists to advance the vision of Kurt Hahn and to support efforts by regional schools to better serve their local community, collaborate effectively, and benefit from strong community relationships and national reach and impact. This network is in turn part of a worldwide network of Outward Bound programs in thirty-three countries, serving more than 250,000 participants annually. Hahn truly birthed a worldwide movement of people committed to serving a greater good.[2]

Outward Bound in the US is committed to helping people face the challenges of the twenty-first century by empowering them to uncover their strengths, confront their fears, and cultivate the qualities that are required of leaders: empathy, compassion, resiliency.

Outward Bound is also committed to developing the best instructors in experiential education: individuals who are fiercely committed to providing participants with a transformative learning experience that inspires them to "do more than they ever thought possible." These are Expeditionary Leaders who internalize the foundational principles: to serve, to strive, and not to yield.

Currently a great emphasis is being placed on character development and social emotional learning across the educational landscape. Outward Bound plays a vital role in developing the "whole child" or the "whole student." For this reason, Outward Bound partners with a growing number of public and private school systems in

---

2. Outward Bound USA's founder, Joshua Minor coauthored *Outward Bound: Crew Not Passengers*, detailing his experiences bringing Kurt Hahn's concepts to the United States.

major US cities such as New York, Boston, Philadelphia, Baltimore, Omaha, and Minneapolis.

Outward Bound recognizes that developing people of moral character cannot be done independently from the other important learning experiences that its participants take part in. For this reason Outward Bound partners with many organizations to deliver on its mission. These collaborations generate custom-designed programs that support a community's needs and learning objectives. Their goal is to tap into and unlock the passions, talents, and energy of a new generation of American youth as they assume positions of leadership. Outward Bound celebrates the many offspring that have spun off from the leaders it has developed.

And while Outward Bound may continually innovate and evolve, it will do so firmly rooted in its core values: integrity, excellence, inclusion, and above all, compassion.

Outward Bound is committed to helping bridge the divides that separate people and groups from one another. Expeditionary Leaders share a common purpose: a commitment to breaking down barriers to opportunity and expanding the experience of transformative education, whether in a school or a board room.

To that end, Outward Bound is developing programs that serve diverse populations such as the national Outward Bound Veterans program; the Police Youth Challenge developed by the Baltimore Chesapeake Bay Outward Bound School, which seeks to uproot biases in the city's police officers and its youth; and the Tribal Youth Partnership Program developed by the Northwest Outward Bound School, which provides pathways for tribal youth to become outdoor educators and gain access to other leadership opportunities within the outdoor industry.

All these new programs—just like the traditional wilderness expeditions for people of all ages and circumstances—are rooted in the idea of developing personal skills and confidence and igniting a spirit of service through adventure and challenge.

What Will These Keys Unlock for You?

Liz Cunningham sees the ability to serve others, strive during adversity, and never yield to uncertainty as the key to riding out the turbulence many of us are feeling about our own future.

> If you treat people with respect, and things start going badly, "OK, it's going badly, but we'll keep on with it. We'll see what happens. "Or if things have gone really badly, "We know we're in a disaster together now, and so we're going to stay tight." Outward Bound reinforces that wisdom. It brings it out into the open in a way that's memorable, that sticks to you.

Those keys change your default settings. If you're in a challenging situation, you now have a template: serve, strive, and do not yield.

"It could be an adventure, even though it's incredibly difficult," Liz said. "Have a sense that this is a shared journey. We're going to work together. There will be incredibly frustrating times. There can be some fantastic times in the middle of a lot of difficulty. That's an incredible template to have imprinted on you."

If you are a current or former Outward Bound staff member, your skills and leadership are critical to our overcoming the challenges we now face. Know that you are uniquely trained and qualified to help lead this evolution during the time of humans. We need you now to serve your communities as the Expeditionary Leaders that you are.

If you are an alumnus of an Outward Bound experience—a wilderness trip, a corporate development program, a peace-building program, a public or private high school or college—if you are among those who have experienced Outward Bound's philosophy, the world is calling you. Our institutions are under more stress than ever before. They need an adept guide—someone who understands that we are far stronger together than apart, that discomfort and adversity can be our greatest teachers, and that we can accomplish great things and overcome seemingly impossible odds when we support each other. They need someone who understands the importance of diversity and inclusivity, the confidence gained through grit and resilience, the great joy of personal mastery, and the inner strength of self-reliance. And above all, our world needs your compassion. Add your stories to the Expeditionary Leaders presented in this book. Know that you have wisdom, knowledge, and skills that few other leaders possess.

If you have not had an Outward Bound experience, I hope you can pull from the lessons of these Expeditionary Leaders: to serve others, to serve a higher calling, and to serve a community; to strive to learn, to strive in adversity, and to strive for your values; and not to yield to uncertainty, not to yield to what is easy, and not to yield to doubt. These are the keys to making a positive impact on your workplace and your community. These lessons are your map and compass to guide you through the future.

It really boils down to two things that are completely enmeshed in the Outward Bound philosophy:

Each of us has way more in us than we realize.
and…
We need each other.

Our schools, communities, organizations, governments, and planet all rely on our interdependence. We can lead from where we are. We don't need the title or position of leader. We just have to do what is right. Despite the risk. For ourselves. For each other.

I opened this book talking about the rapid change and disruption that our planet and our societies are facing. The speed of change often leaves us reeling, and it sometimes seems as if humanity is suffering from vertigo. Keeping up with the speed of change feels impossible. We can feel overwhelmed and disempowered.

As Peace Corps and Outward Bound pioneer Richard Holzman so aptly stated, in this digital age we are more connected than ever, but many feel a great sense of disconnection and dis-ease. Not just in the United States, but across the globe, we are experiencing the upheaval caused by this sense of isolation: the rise of nationalism and populism, the marginalization of displaced people, and the apparent polarities that are magnified by social media.

Outward Bound was born during a similar time of great upheaval and turmoil. It was designed to help wayfarers develop the confidence and resilience to overcome any challenge—and to do that by supporting others and serving the greater good.

These stories are representative of the hundreds of thousands of people who have become Expeditionary Leaders by supporting others and serving the greater good. Even if this is your first exposure to Outward Bound, you too have been given the keys through these lessons. It is time for you to use them.

Outward Bound's name is a nautical term. When a ship is venturing to sea, the captain raises a blue peter flag (Outward Bound's adopted symbol), signifying that the ship leaving the harbor is "outward bound." Yes, ships in the harbor are safe. But that's not what ships are for. They are meant to be outward bound.

About the Expeditionary Leaders

I am grateful to the people who shared their stories with me as I developed this book. They represent the thousands of former instructors and alumni whose lives were shaped by Outward Bound. Many others also helped and supported me on the journey of creating this book. In particular, I am grateful for the support of Whitney Montgomery and the North Carolina Outward Bound School leadership, who helped make connections to many of the leaders profiled. I am immensely grateful to Patricia Woodson, who opened doors for me with many of the people and programs that helped shape this book. I am particularly grateful also to Amanda Osmer and her late brother, Greg Grappone. Both attended Outward Bound courses and invited me to join them in transforming their company, the Grappone Automotive Group, using Expeditionary Leadership and Outward Bound principles. Unfortunately, we lost Greg to cancer, but I knew he would be excited to see where his family's company has ventured.

Peter Bailey

Peter is the president of the Prouty Project, which delivers strategic planning and leadership development programs to organizations worldwide. Prior to joining the Prouty Project, Peter worked for Wilson Learning as a global performance consultant, where he was a writer, designer, and lead facilitator focusing on global effectiveness.

Peter was introduced to Outward Bound almost by happenstance. Early in his career he joined an organization called Urban Adventures, which prepares students from the South Bronx to attend Outward Bound summer expeditions. Greg Farrell, who served on the board of Urban Adventures, was selected to manage a fund set up to launch an Urban Outward Bound Center in New York City, the first in the United States. The new Outward Bound program was housed at the headquarters of Urban Adventures, and Peter by default became one of the first urban Outward Bound instructors in the country. Peter relocated to the Twin Cities and helped launch some of the first educational reform programs in the country using Outward Bound principles in the classroom through the Voyageur Outward Bound School. He is currently on the board of trustees of the Voyageur Outward Bound School.

Eduardo Balarezo

Eduardo is a financier, business leader, and social entrepreneur. He led several companies in Ecuador and Peru, including Peruval SAC as managing partner, Grupo Aries as executive vice president, and Abingdon SA as president and cofounder.

Eduardo took Outward Bound to Ecuador in 2006 and served as president for five years. He has also served on the board of Outward Bound International. A serial entrepreneur, Eduardo emigrated to the United States in 2012, launching the social retail enterprise

Lonesome George & Co. to benefit the Galápagos Islands. He also launched the Academy of Agents of Change, a unique education approach based on Outward Bound principles and social entrepreneurship. Eduardo recently founded Mind Shift Impact, a transformational consulting company based on Expeditionary Leadership principles.

Luis Benitez

Luis is the vice president of government affairs and global impact for VF Corporation. Prior to that he was the first director of the Colorado Outdoor Recreation Industry Office. Created in 2015, the office focuses on four areas of the outdoor recreation industry: economic development, education and workforce training, conservation and stewardship, and health and wellness.

Luis began working for the Colorado Outward Bound School as a teenager, eventually becoming involved in facilitating leadership- and team-building programs with Outward Bound's corporate branch, Outward Bound Professional. He is one of the world's foremost mountaineers and guides, having summited six of the famed "seven summits" thirty-two times. He has reached the summit of Mount Everest six times; his experience leading blind mountaineer Eric Weihenmayer's successful climb was featured in the film *Farther Than the Eye Can See.*

Arthur Blank

Along with his partner, Bernard Marcus, Arthur cofounded The Home Depot in 1978. The company revolutionized the home improvement industry and became the largest home improvement retailer in the United States. Arthur spent nineteen years as president before succeeding his business partner as CEO. Arthur brought

Outward Bound's philosophy into the strategy of The Home Depot to develop strong Expeditionary Leaders as company rapidly grew. In 2001 Arthur retired from The Home Depot. His business holdings now include the Atlanta Falcons, the Atlanta United professional soccer team, PGA Tour Superstores, Mercedes-Benz stadium management, and the Mountain Sky guest ranch in Montana.

Arthur became involved with Outward Bound through one of his early investors, Marjorie Bryan Buckley, who is a founder and life director of the North Carolina Outward Bound School. Arthur has served and chaired the boards of both the North Carolina Outward Bound School and Outward Bound USA and is a life director of NCOBS.

Arthur's intense care for the community has become the greatest focus of his legacy work. Founded in 1995, the Arthur M. Blank Family Foundation has invested more than $360 million in early childhood development, education, greenspace, community transformation, and the arts.

Liz Cunningham

Liz is an author, speaker, and conservationist. Her career began as a political journalist, but she changed direction dramatically after a kayaking accident nearly killed her. She was temporarily paralyzed from the waist down and spent nearly a decade healing. During that time, she decided to dedicate her life to protecting the seas. Her book *Ocean Country* chronicled her travels around the world exploring protected marine areas and sustainable fisheries.

Liz first experienced Outward Bound as a teenager on a course in North Carolina, but she was already well indoctrinated in its philosophy. Her great-uncle was Kurt Hahn, the founder of Outward Bound, and her early memories of him and his approach to life greatly shaped her commitment to helping protect the world's oceans and making the world a better place. Liz is currently writing a book, *The Passion for Rescue, the Heart of Hope,* based on Hahn's beliefs that service to others is the highest form of compassion.

Maggie Fox

Maggie Fox is a consultant working with organizations, foundations, and communities focused on climate change and clean-energy strategies. She is the past president and CEO of The Climate Reality Project and The Climate Action Fund. She also served as the president of America Votes and deputy executive director of the Sierra Club. She has spent her entire career helping to protect our natural world.

Maggie came to Outward Bound first as a participant. She was one of the first female instructors in the Outward Bound system and worked at both the North Carolina and Colorado Outward Bound schools. Along with her husband, Mark Udall, she has also been on mountaineering expeditions around the world.

Richard Holzman

Richard is the senior adviser for the University of Massachusetts Amherst's College of Education. He spent nearly his entire career in education working as a high school superintendent, graduate dean, and professor. Richard has the distinction of participating in the first Outward Bound experience in the United States as part of the inaugural class of JFK's Peace Corps.

Richard was one of the first to adapt experiential learning principles as a precursor for Outward Bound's educational reforms. He has served on several different Outward Bound organizations and continues to give his time to civic groups near his home in western Massachusetts.

Thomas James

Dr. Thomas James is the provost and dean of the Teachers College at Columbia University. He has been involved with Outward Bound for more than forty years and is considered one of the most knowledgeable authorities on Kurt Hahn and Outward Bound.

In 2016 Thomas received the Kurt Hahn award. Named in honor of Outward Bound's founder, the award is presented annually to a person who exemplifies outstanding service to Outward Bound's mission to change lives through challenge and discovery and to create a more resilient and compassionate world. Thomas helped establish the New York City Outward Bound Center and has served on the board of Outward Bound for many years.

Laura Kohler

Laura has held numerous positions during her twenty-six-year career at her family's privately held business, Kohler Co. Currently she leads the worldwide human resources function for Kohler, which employs more than thirty-five thousand people across the globe. In addition, Laura oversees the global social impact team, which focuses on environmental sustainability, corporate stewardship, and innovation for good initiatives. She serves on the Kohler corporate board of directors as well as the boards of the John Michael Kohler Arts Center and The Actors Center in New York City. She is also board chair for the Kohler Trust for the Arts and Education and for the Kohler Trust for Preservation.

Laura experienced Outward Bound first as a participant on a mountaineering course with the Pacific Crest Outward Bound School as a teenager. She returned to Outward Bound as an instructor for Voyageur Outward Bound School's urban programs in Chicago and worked as a wilderness instructor for the Voyageur school in Montana. Laura has served as the board chair of Outward Bound USA, becoming one of the first former instructors to help guide the federation of schools.

Rue Mapp

Rue is the founder of Outdoor Afro, the nation's leading network celebrating and inspiring African American connections and leadership in nature. With more than seventy leaders in thirty states, Outdoor Afro connects thousands of people to outdoor experiences. In 2010 Rue was invited to the White House to participate in the America's Great Outdoors conference and was later asked to join a think tank tasked with helping to create the first lady's "Let's Move" initiative. In 2014 Governor Jerry Brown appointed Rue to the California State Parks Commission.

Rue participated in an Outward Bound course in the Southern Sierra in California. Her story of Outward Bound's impact has become part of her organization's creation story, and she shares it with groups across the United States. Rue has also received numerous awards for her groundbreaking work, including the Root 100 as one of the most influential African Americans in the country, the Outdoor Industry Inspiration Award, and the National Wildlife Federation Communications Award.

Delaney Reynolds

Delaney is the founder of the Sink or Swim Project, a nonprofit focused on advocacy and education around the impact of climate change and sea-level rise around the globe. Delaney has given a popular TEDx talk and appeared on several television shows, including National Geographic Channel's *Years of Living Dangerously* with Jack Black (also an Outward Bound alumnus), *Xploration*

Awesome Planet on Fox with Philippe Cousteau, and MTV's "An Inconvenient Special" town hall with former vice president Al Gore. Delaney has also addressed the General Assembly of the United Nations on climate change and serves on several advisory boards, representing the youth vote. She has been honored with the inaugural National Geographic Teen Service Award, the *Miami Herald*'s Silver Knight Award for Social Science, the University of Rochester George Eastman Young Leader's Award, the Gloria Barron Prize for Young Heroes, and the University of Miami's Singer Scholarship and Foote Fellowship.

Delaney launched her nonprofit while in high school and is now studying marine biology at the University of Miami's Rosenstiel School of Marine and Atmospheric Science. She is the author of several children's books and is currently writing a book that reflects the impact of sea rise on her home in South Florida. Delaney was introduced to Outward Bound through her high school, attending her first course in the Everglades. She has completed multiple expeditions as part of her education and credits Outward Bound with helping her find her voice and her confidence to make a difference in the world.

Paul "Pablo" Stayton

Pablo is the dean of faculty and a humanities educator at the Watershed School in Boulder, Colorado. Pablo joined the staff of the Voyageur Outward Bound School after graduating from Earlham College. He has more than 1,200 days in the field, leading trips in Minnesota, Montana, Arizona, Texas, and Colorado. Pablo has also led international and cross-cultural trips to Ojinaga and the Copper Canyon in Mexico, and to Guatemala, Nicaragua, Costa Rica, and China.

Pablo became the program director for the Rio Grande base camp for Voyageur Outward Bound and also oversaw the opening of programming in the Gila Wilderness Area in New Mexico and Arizona. He also served as the Voyageur School program director, overseeing the safety and operations of programs in Minnesota, Canada, Montana, New Mexico, Arizona, Texas and Mexico.

Mark Udall

Mark has served as a member of the US Senate and House, representing Colorado, and as a state representative, representing Boulder. Throughout his career Mark championed renewable energy, protection for national parks and wilderness areas, and support for our armed services.

Mark was raised in an environment of adventure, with the summers of his youth spent exploring the canyon country and mountains of the Four Corners. During a January break in college he persuaded his adviser to allow him to attend a winter mountaineering course with Outward Bound, and he was hooked. After college he began working at the Colorado Outward Bound School and, after a decade of fieldwork, became the program's executive director. He led the school during "the golden time" of Outward Bound's expansion, overseeing programs in multiple states as well as abroad.

Michael Welp

Michael has spent the past thirty-plus years working with leadership teams around the world. He is the author of *Four Days to Change* and cofounder of a diversity and inclusion consulting company, White Men as Full Diversity Partners. Challenging the traditional male-dominated approach to doing business, WMFDP is one of the only organizations focused on helping white men learn to create a more inclusive environment.

Michael, who now has a PhD, was pursuing an undergraduate degree in engineering when he encountered some Outward Bound instructors at a retreat; it opened his eyes to a world he never knew existed. He switched his major to psychology but took a break to join Outward Bound as a wilderness instructor, working for the Voyageur School in northern Minnesota. He obtained a graduate degree in organizational development at American University in Washington, D.C., where he was exposed to diversity issues for the first time. This was the beginning of his Expeditionary Leadership, where he began searching for a way to blend his love of experiential learning and diversity.

Patricia Woodson

Patricia cocreated the first online marketplace for professional photography, Photo.net. She served as president and CEO of the company, which she sold after twelve years. Patricia has since worked as an executive coach and served as a city commissioner for Key Biscayne, Florida. She is an advocate for the protection of the environment and cofounded a Citizen Scientist project, a partnership between the University of Miami, the local community foundation, and the village of Key Biscayne.

Patricia has served on the board of the North Carolina Outward Bound School and currently serves as the school's director of advancement for Florida. She was one of the first female Outward Bound instructors, leading mountaineering courses. She and her daughters administer a family fund in honor of her mother, Dicie Woodson, an educator who devoted her life to improving education and literacy.

Acknowledgments

The seeds for this book were first planted while I was in graduate school at Western Carolina University in 2005. I had at that point been involved with Outward Bound for nearly two decades, and during a semester on organizational and entrepreneurial leadership, I wrote a paper titled "Beyond Competition: Expeditionary Leadership and the Transformation of Organizations." This was the beginning of my examination of the true impact that Outward Bound has had on the world.

After joining the Grappone Automotive Group in 2012, I once again pulled out the concept and began exploring whether I could turn it into a book. Then two things happened that really set this book in motion. First, Richard Leider, the author and master coach who so kindly wrote the foreword for this book, spent an hour or so on the phone with me and reignited both my passion for Outward Bound and my desire to write. Richard was an Outward Bound board member, and I had always deeply admired him and his work. His encouragement helped me refocus my energy on telling this story. Second, I ended up sitting next to Neal Maillet, editorial director of Berrett-Koehler Publishers at a Conscious Capitalism conference. After listening to my story, he encouraged me to reach out to Outward Bound and offered to help shepherd me through the proposal process. Without the support of these two, this book would have never happened. To the both of them I offer my deepest gratitude.

Thank you to the Expeditionary Leaders featured in this book for your willingness to share your stories. You have my deepest respect and appreciation. To the Outward Bound communities I lived and worked with at Homeplace in Minnesota and Redford, Texas, during my years as a wilderness instructor: thank you. I miss you and those days more than I could ever express. You are the best people I have ever known. Thanks to Bob Stout and Bill Murray at the North Carolina Outward Bound School, who always respected my creativity and allowed me to develop many of the concepts that underpin this book. Thanks to Amy Saxton Mason for helping me with the initial connections with Outward Bound USA, Penny Jeffers for helping to shepherd the early conversations on the book, and Peter Steinhauser at Outward Bound for supporting this project wholeheartedly and helping guide it every step of the way.

Thanks to Joel Arndt, Lisa Ramsay, and Sarah Wallace, who said yes to my call for readers and offered great feedback on helping better shape the manuscript. Thank you to my editor Danielle Goodman, who worked wonders in pulling out the lessons and bringing them to the forefront. You are amazing! To my wonderfully supportive wife, Mandy, who read and edited the manuscript, put up with my daily rising at 4 a.m. to write, and who has always encouraged me to pursue my crazy dreams: thank you. For my son, Noah: I want you to know that you can accomplish anything if you dedicate yourself to it. And finally, I dedicate this to the memory of three

Outward Bound leaders who challenged me, shaped me, and left this world much too soon: Jack Willis, Paul Smith, and Don "Opie" Opert. I stand on the shoulders of these giants.

Index

About the Author

Mark M. Brown grew up in northeastern Ohio. After graduating from the University of Akron with a degree in communication he relocated to Naples, Florida, working as a magazine editor, public relations consultant, and freelance writer. Finding himself burned out at the ripe old age of twenty-five and longing for a bit of adventure, he heeded the advice of friends and attended a twenty-three-day Outward Bound course in Utah. The trip was life changing.

Mark's career with Outward Bound began after he showed up for a visit at Homeplace, an OB base in northern Minnesota. He was hired to drive a van. On the eve of this temporary job's final day, a teenage boy became separated from his group and Mark was pulled into a three-day search. The boy was found unharmed, though bug bitten and very hungry. Outward Bound then asked Mark to stay and train to become an instructor.

Mark spent the next decade working for the Voyageur Outward Bound School, spending six months a year leading canoe expeditions in the Boundary Waters in northern Minnesota and Canada and six months leading whitewater paddling, canyoneering and desert backpacking courses in the Big Bend region of West Texas and northern Mexico. He became a course director and later program manager for a twenty-eight-day at-risk youth program and eventually moved to Minneapolis to open a group sales department for Outward Bound.

Mark relocated to Asheville, North Carolina, and continued his work with the North Carolina Outward Bound School. He trained to be a professional coach and began designing some of the first corporate leadership development programs that Outward Bound offered, blending the wilderness with classroom training and organizational consulting.

Mark and his wife launched their own coaching, training, and facilitation business, which they ran for nearly a decade. Along the way he earned a master's degree in business/entrepreneurship from Western Carolina University, and he and his wife welcomed their son Noah into the world.

In 2012 Mark was invited to join the leadership of a privately held company. As the director of corporate potential, he launched a program to guide the company through the most significant culture change in its more than 90-year history and garnered national recognition for its unique way of doing business.

This is Mark's first book. He continues his work as a master coach, consultant, and facilitator, helping people and organizations navigate the rapid changes of our modern world. You can learn more about the Expeditionary Leadership process at Mark's website, www.markmbrown.com. When not working you'll most likely find Mark disappearing down a trail or paddling a canoe somewhere. The wilderness always calls!

Berrett–Koehler
BK Publishers

Berrett-Koehler is an independent publisher dedicated to an ambitious mission: *Connecting people and ideas to create a world that works for all.*

Our publications span many formats, including print, digital, audio, and video. We also offer online resources, training, and gatherings. And we will continue expanding our products and services to advance our mission.

We believe that the solutions to the world's problems will come from all of us, working at all levels: in our society, in our organizations, and in our own lives. Our publications and resources offer pathways to creating a more just, equitable, and sustainable society. They help people make their organizations more humane, democratic, diverse, and effective (and we don't think there's any contradiction there). And they guide people in creating positive change in their own lives and aligning their personal practices with their aspirations for a better world.

And we strive to practice what we preach through what we call "The BK Way." At the core of this approach is *stewardship,* a deep sense of responsibility to administer the company for the benefit of all of our stakeholder groups, including authors, customers, employees, investors, service providers, sales partners, and the communities and environment around us. Everything we do is built around stewardship and our other core values of *quality, partnership, inclusion,* and *sustainability.*

This is why Berrett-Koehler is the first book publishing company to be both a B Corporation (a rigorous certification) and a benefit corporation (a for-profit legal status), which together require us to adhere to the highest standards for corporate, social, and environmental performance. And it is why we have instituted many pioneering practices (which you can learn about at www.bkconnection.com), including the Berrett-Koehler Constitution, the Bill of Rights and Responsibilities for BK Authors, and our unique Author Days.

We are grateful to our readers, authors, and other friends who are supporting our mission. We ask you to share with us examples of how BK publications and resources are making a difference in your lives, organizations, and communities at www.bkconnection.com/impact.

Dear reader,

Thank you for picking up this book and welcome to the worldwide BK community! You're joining a special group of people who have come together to create positive change in their lives, organizations, and communities.

What's BK all about?

Our mission is to connect people and ideas to create a world that works for all.

Why? Our communities, organizations, and lives get bogged down by old paradigms of self-interest, exclusion, hierarchy, and privilege. But we believe that can change. That's why we seek the leading experts on these challenges—and share their actionable ideas with you.

A welcome gift

To help you get started, we'd like to offer you a **free copy** of one of our bestselling ebooks:

www.bkconnection.com/welcome

When you claim your **free ebook**, you'll also be subscribed to our blog.

Our freshest insights

Access the best new tools and ideas for leaders at all levels on our blog at ideas.bkconnection.com.

Sincerely,

Your friends at Berrett-Koehler